GW00536367

CRASH THE ASH

Some Joy for the Beleaguered Smoker

filtered by

AUBERON WAUGH

'What did I tell you about smoking in front of the Minister, darling?'

Quiller Press London

© 1994 Quiller Press Limited
© illustrations – individuals as acknowledged
First published 1994 by
Quiller Press Ltd
46 Lillie Road
London SW6 1ND

No part of this book may be reproduced by
any means without permission of the Publishers.

ISBN 1 870948 95 5

Front cover by Tim Jaques
Book design by Tim McPhee
Produced by Book Production Consultants Plc
25 - 27 High Street, Chesterton, Cambridge CB4 1ND
Printed by Redwood Books, Trowbridge, Wiltshire

CRASH THE ASH

Some Joy for the Beleaguered Smoker

Contents

'Let's face it, passive smoking was a stupid choice of weapon!'

Introduction

BY AUBERON WAUGH

When I was first asked to get involved with this book I imagined it would be some sort of Smokers' Commonplace Book, with colour plates of seventeeth- and eighteenth-century men smoking clay pipes, rare and unusual smokers' implements and learned essays on the cultivation of tobacco. It would be a coffee table book to be admired from a distance but scarcely read, rather than one of those books to be read in the train, discussed in the pub and chortled over in the smallest room.

In the event the collection does indeed provide a bewildering variety of unexpected and unusual facts of interest to the smoker. This above all provides a good-natured polemic whose most useful function will be to cheer us up in the struggle against the forces of puritanism and oppression – for which smokers have much to thank "Colonel Puffer", whose words link most of the material under my gaze.

I speak of a struggle, but of course it is entirely one-sided. There is effectively no resistance to the oppression because we are all ashamed of our pleasures. Since the invention of passive smoking as a health hazard, it may seem that the smoker does not have a leg to stand on. Even if he had ever been able to assemble the smallest tithe of his opponent's moral righteousness in defence of his private pleasures, his case was lost now.

This book does not intend to set out the technical reasons for believing that the passive smoking scare is one of the biggest lies foisted on the public by health fanatics in the history of health fanaticism. Perhaps it is not even fair to see it as a lie, although I think it comes quite close to that. When I was a child, health fanatics made every British schoolboy and schoolgirl drink a bottle of disgusting pasteurised milk every day. Then they decided that milk was the worst possible thing for us to drink, filling us with fatty cholesterols. Next they told us to eat margarine and never drink more than one glass of wine a day, then only if we were desperate. Next thing we hear is that margarine is deadly poison, and anyone who does not drink at least a bottle of red wine every day is heading for the scrapheap.

But these are incidental blunders, arising from the health fiend's simple desire to torment and boss us around. They were never deliberate lies in the way that such lies are told by those who see themselves as having a sacred duty to stop everyone smoking. No doubt the reason why anti-smokists feel free to distort figures, manufacture facts and ignore contrary evidence is because they feel they know, as some of us think we know, that there is a germ of truth at the centre of it. Smoking is not good for the health (although it can have many salutary properties in the fields of releasing tension, encouraging mental tranquility and concentration) and perhaps it can be very bad for the health. It is said that some smokers die, on average, two or three years younger than non-smokers, although it is certainly not true that all smokers die young. We are reminded of Compton Mackenzie, who regarded tobacco as the hand-maiden of literature, and died after writing nearly a hundred books, universally loved, at the age of 89. The great P.G. Wodehouse, who died at 94 in 1975, remarked in an autobiography written nearly 25 years earlier that the forces of darkness were gathering strength in their struggle to stop people like himself enjoying a quiet smoke.

It is perhaps because the forces of darkness have a tiny scintilla of truth at their disposal that they feel justified in supporting their case with distortions of the truth and plain untruths. Statistics are thrown around with total abandon and figures are given for alleged deaths from so-called smoking-related diseases which include all deaths from respiratory or circulatory causes. We are told that smoking-related diseases cost the National Health Service so many million pounds a year, when the truth of the matter is that the smoker, by the extra taxes he pays in Excise Duty and VAT, pays many times that invented sum – in fact smokers at £4 million every day pay for a quarter of the cost of the entire NHS.

Perhaps the most bare-faced lie I came across in many years of following these things was when British Rail stopped selling cigarettes on trains (it still sells them at stations) and gave us its reason that there was no demand for them. So many fewer people were smoking nowadays, they said, that the demand had dried up. These anti-smokers live in a funny little world of their own, telling each other these lies until they come to believe them. Their campaigns typically start by being half admirable, rapidly proceed to bring foolish and end by being dangerously unpleasant as intelligence gives way to a ranting form of political correctness.

Beside the Big Lie about passive smoking as a serious health hazard, these little lies of the single issue fanatics pale into insignificance. The most important thing at a time when smokers are being turned into social lepers is that

The real reason dinosaurs became extinct

we should determinedly see the smoker as a heroic figure. This book would make a suitable prize for heroism, given by smokers to each other and by non-smokers to smokers in gratitude and admiration for their efforts. Smokers are heroes in the first place because they pay an enormous amount of extra tax which non-smokers do not pay (the same, of course, is true of drinkers and non-drinkers) and thus make a significant contribution to the welfare of everyone else. If people deny that they receive any benefit from the government, at least smokers save them having to pay extra tax for the government to pay its own wages and the wages of its 5.2 million more or less redundant employees.

In the second place, smokers are heroes precisely because they do – die, if indeed they do, on average, two or three years younger. They do not then clutter up the welfare services, nor put a terrible burden on their children, nor spend everything they have to leave on nursing home fees. Longevity is becoming the great curse of western civilisation. At its worst manifestation, there are wards and wards where old people lie in semi-coma, usually on a drip, recognizing nobody, understanding nothing, being turned three times a day like damp hay. That is the end-product of all the moral righteousness of the health fascists. Of course these people, like that great anti-smoker Adolf Hitler, also think morality is on their side. Smokers have none of these airy fairy notions. They just believe that life is to be enjoyed. I hope this book helps them to enjoy it a little more.

Please Smoke

this is a smoking area

If you persist in not smoking
you may be requested to leave

1

BECAUSE THEY LIKE IT - *Ladies first*

Powder Puff, Ciggy Puff, Bonk

'It was disgusting - they had a cigarette afterwards.'

Powder Puff, Bonk, Ciggy Puff

When all is ~~said~~ done and done,
it's all much of
a muchness.

Blackpool

The strain of the change of lifestyle from kipping down with her, to keeping up with her, is relieved by resigned, submissive smoking, while dreaming of what he considers THE REAL ME IF ONLY.

But when the holiday is over he knows he must return to the real Real Me which is trotting every morning down Acacia Avenue to catch the 8.20.

But having no pipe to draw on has its drawbacks, as SHE well knows

'Why don't you start smoking and then quit so you'd have an excuse for your testiness.'

THE CAFE PROPRIETOR CAN SHUNT HIM OFF INTO HIS OWN COMPARTMENT

WORRY-FREE WEEKEND

MONDAY TO FRIDAY is one thing, but Saturday to Sunday it is a matter of getting behind with the mowing while SHE gets ahead with getting up to date on who's been doing what and for how long with THAT ONE NEXT DOOR.

But HE's not one to let the grass grow under his feet. It provides him with a welcome moment - left leg crossing his right in a casual carry-on-what-have-I-to-lose? pose - for a nonchalant puff or two, or three or thirteen, at his Hamlet.

At least that nice Dr Groper appreciates her, even if Supercilious Sam doesn't

Momma doesn't mind Sam smoking, just the smirk on his face while he's puffing away while he waits for her to hear the *full* story of what Mabel is supposed to have done with the raffle takings.

In her attitude to the so-called 'dangers' of what Mrs C, for some reason she can't understand, calls 'passive smoking' - 'I don't smoke Mrs C, what makes you say I'm a passive smoker ?' - she is the latest in a line of women stretching back to the eighteenth century and longer, like Parson Woodforde's friend Mrs Custance.

She LIKES it

When in April 1785 Parson Woodforde, rector of Weston Longeville in Norfolk, received a visit from his friend Mrs Custance, he was smoking his Afternoon Pipe. He had not finished when he heard the knock on the door. Fearing she would object to it he put it aside. But, he wrote in his diary,

'I told Mrs Custance that I had been smoking and hoped she did not dislike it - and she said she liked it.'

Women who drag on a miserable life Without tobacco are to be pitied

PARSON WOODFORDE does not record whether Mrs Custance, who had no objection to second-hand tobacco smoke, ever smoked a pipe herself, although many of her sex did so, rarely in public however. In 1715 a lady who considered tobacco to be the secret of long life, wrote a short book with a long title:

A SOUND AND PLEASANT PROOF that a Respectable Woman may sometimes enter a Coffee House without damage to her Good Name, and moreover she may and should treat herself to a Pipe of Tobacco

It was a glorious venture, wrote a German doctor from Leipzig thirty years later, when a woman took heart to smoke a pipe of tobacco. Tobacco was invaluable, he wrote, 'I pity those who drag on a miserable life without it.'

Madame Vigée-Lebrun (1755-1842) smoking

For these women a box of cigarettes was more prized than a box of chocs.

“ SIR WALTER RALEIGH AND SIR FRANCIS DRAKE, who popularized this strange habit of smoking first introduced into England, direct from America, by Sir John Hawkins in 1565, had doubtless many admirers among the fair sex, who were not loath to follow a fashion set by such public idols as the grave sea-dogs. On the Continent, even more than in this country, smoking by women has never been regarded as unwomanly or out of place; the women of Russia, China, Siam, Turkey and the East generally set more store by a box of cigarettes than the Western women do by their box of chocolates. ”

(*B.A.T. Bulletin*, 1928)

Not all that Thoroughly MODERN *Millies*

Thoroughly Modern Millies working for the British-American Tobacco Company - 'shingled, powdered and lip-salved, short-skirted, Charleston-stepping flappers' - who read that piece in their *B.A.T. Bulletin* in the nineteen twenties also learnt from the same article that there was a time when several women were publicly knouted in Russia for what was a punishable offence. The BAT girls should be glad they were living in 1928 and not 1628.

> So the modern Young Thing, boldly lighting a cigarette in tram, theatre or restaurant, and smoking it in an attitude suggesting defiance of anything so out of date as yesterday's paper, is not so excessively modern after all, since her ancestors of three hundred years ago did the same thing with considerably less defiance about it !

If they had read on, their morale would have been restored by hearing that during the Great Plague of 1665 smoking was a life-saver. They were considered immune from dying the black death. It was a time when it was usual, not only for women to join the men in smoking but, as one John Ashton wrote, 'in Worcestershire the children were sent to school with pipes in their satchels, and the schoolmaster called a halt in their studies while they all smoked.'

Red Smoke Gets In Your Eyes

← If this picture was in colour you would see that the smoke coming from her cigarette was red to match the red of the lacquer on her fingernails, the red of her lipstick, the roses in her hat, the voile round her shoulders, the bow at her bosom and - approximately - the red Bordeaux in that bottle and in her glass.

Coloured cigarette smoke had been invented by an American from Tennessee called Otto Miller who patented it in ten shades.

Now there's an idea for a thoroughly modern manufacturer to take up in 1995 !

COLOURED SMOKE ?

COLOURED TIP
IF NOT COLOURED SMOKE

Alfred Hedges made miniature 'Cigarette Turc' cigarettes for ladies tipped with either parma violet petals or Marechal Niel rose petals 'plucked with the morning dew on them.' He had them packed in gaily coloured boxes. Furthermore, if any of their fair clients wanted it, Mr Hedges and Mr Benson would have the ladies' initials printed on each cigarette and, for those who could rustle up a family crest, that as well.

Her ladyship anticipates disappointment

IN THE EIGHTEEN NINETIES, according to one Lady Greville who wrote a book on etiquette called *The Gentlewoman in Society*, ladies were daringly imitating the male habit of smoking in the dining room after the ladies had left, and 'the silver cigarette box and the dainty spirit lamp wherewith to light it are passed round'.

But she saw it creating problems.

> Think of the disappointment of the ardent lover when, pressing the lips of his adored one, he finds upon them the flavour of an inferior quality of tobacco !

The romance would go up in smoke. But bad, she felt, could only go to worse.

> Ladies will surely not stop short at cigarettes; they will require shilling cigars until eventually, perhaps, they may, from motives of economy, even take to the 'churchwarden'. (1892)

She had obviously not heard of Madame Lebrun.

'Smoking or nonsmoking, cholesterol or non-cholesterol, caffeinated or decaffeinated?'

But never in her wildest dreams did she think this could happen.

Would Lady Greville have approved of this?

Patience Humphry of Honiton.

WITH THIS ARTISTIC trade card of elegantly dressed tobacconists – as the smokers of tobacco were once called – resting their feet on a barrel of rum (?) in their favourite tavern, Patience Humphry gave herself a high-class image, as a creme-de-la-creme Lady Tobacconiste. Incidentally, the OED says the word 'tobacconist' in 1657 meant a dealer or manufacturer of tobacco; and in 1757 a user of tobacco. Patience probably did both – smoked and sold.

BUT JUST WHAT this good woman is doing is anybody's guess. Call that smoking? She'd need a lot of patience to get any pleasure out of *that* contraption. In the Transvaal, where this trade mark comes from, they obviously did it their way, and liked it their way.

THE LONE MAN'S COMPANION

THE AUTHOR OF *The Gentlewoman in Society* forecast that the day would come when a man handed his partner (his dance partner, that is) a cigarette as naturally as a strawberry ice. Doubtless it would become The Thing that the first present which a happy bridegroom gave his bride was a cigarette box and a match box.

IF THE TREND which Lady Greville feared was allowed to develop, it would seem that tobacco would become a ladies' companion as well as 'the lone man's companion', the description given to it by one widely read novelist who had one of his characters praise it as

> a bachelor's friend, a hungry man's food, a sad man's cordial, a wakeful man's sleep, and a chilly man's fire ... there's no herb like unto it under the canopy of heaven. (Charles Kingsley, *Westward Ho!* 1855)

Placing Licensed Sex on a Pedestal

WHAT WAS DISGUSTING to our Victorian grandmothers and grandfathers was not cigarette *smoking* – in bed or out of bed – but cigarette *cards.*

An outraged reader of *The Times* wrote to the editor in 1894 accusing the tobacco companies, not of harming the nation's health but, with their licentious cigarette cards of pretty girls, "placing licensed sex on a pedestal".

***Protopapas's* Beauties.**

***Egyptian Cigarette Company's* Beauties.**

Another letter-writer saw the wicked pictures as "corrupting the morals of the younger generation"; a third as "a form of sexual excitement to induce moral degeneration in the male".

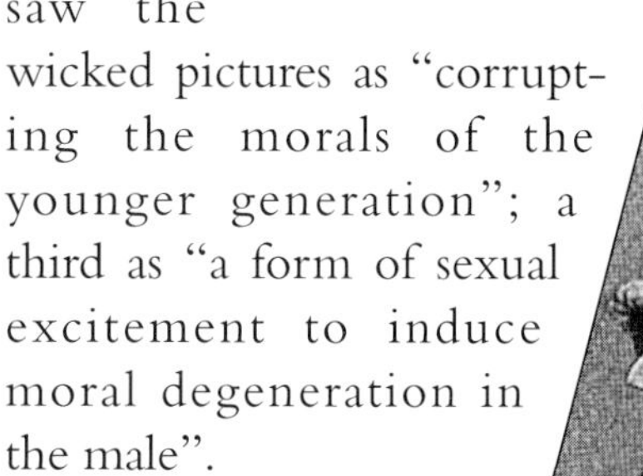

Baker's series of *Beauties of All Nations,* Adkin's *Actresses and Pretty Girls,* and Wills's *Actresses and Beauties* were seen as particularly corrupting.

Whoops-a-Daisy!

THEN THE *Gents*

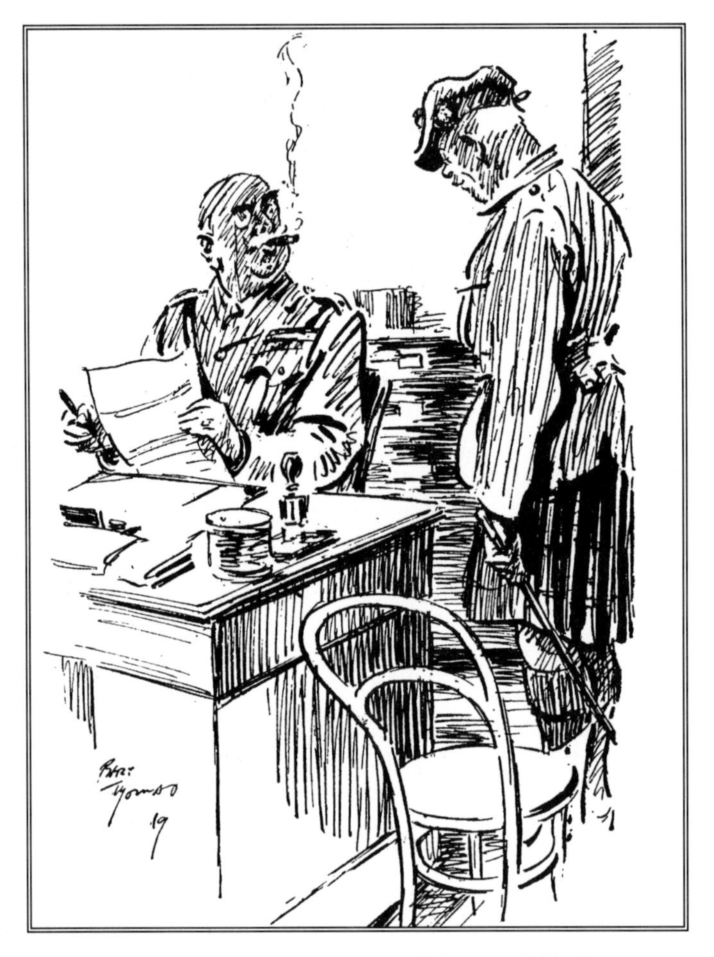

Why am I smoking this cigar ? Because I like it.
Why are you wearing that skirt ?

Not always a cigar.
In civvies he thinks it suits him
better to sport a meerschaum...

It's always been their pleasure

IN WHATEVER CENTURY, however dressed, hatted or bare-headed, with friends or alone, standing or sitting, talking or thinking, smoking has always been done, and is still being done, purely for pleasure.

MANY OF THOSE GIFTED with the powers of expression have described the delight they get from it.

J B PRIESTLEY (1894-1984) in 1949 published in a limited edition a book of essays he called *Delight*. In one of them on smoking he wrote that he had been doing so since 1910. Thirty years later he was preserving the 1910 spirit in smoking, 'for in those days tobacco was not sold by young women lost in the myths of Hollywood but by solid middle-aged men' who pulled down their canisters of Old Virginia, Perique and Latakia and mixed you something new on the spot if necessary and 'lived with you in a community of palates'.

IN A LETTER written in 1951 which American Tom Dunn published in his *Pipe Smokers' Ephemeris* in 1993, Priestley confessed to having forty to fifty pipes, mostly briars.

Turkish Delight - two-handed style

THE PIPE SMOKER'S EPHEMERIS

TOM DUNN
Editor / Publisher

20-37 120th Street, College Point, N.Y. 11356 U.S.A.

Volcanic Delight

The prolific writer Compton Mackenzie (1883-1972), pictured right, declared in 1957, in a book which was his eighty-first, that 'without being a smoker I doubt if I should have written half that number.' He knew that at the age of 74 he could not be penning what he was writing at three o'clock in the morning, after ten hours of work unbroken except by the briefest dinner and listening to music while he smoked a small cigar, unless he had been sustained by pipe after pipe. He reckoned that in the course of his life he had smoked 200,000 pipefuls of tobacco at the very least, and probably nearer a quarter of a million. The volume of smoke from those pipes might not disgrace the volcano Vesuvius when not in full eruption.

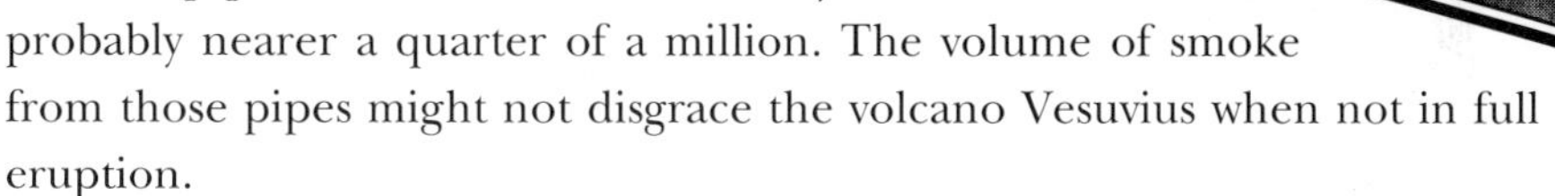

Damp Delight

A Cigarette Makes Utter Strangers Disposed to Friendliness

Compton Mackenzie knew with absolute certainty that the harder he worked the more he needed to smoke because, he said, tobacco was the handmaiden of literature. He would argue stoutly that every man, whatever his race, whatever his rank, whatever his profession, whatever his work, was helped by smoking.

As someone who was not a regular cigarette smoker, he admitted to being insufficiently aware of the predominant part that cigarettes played in the pleasure of contemporary smoking.

However he recognised that the vast majority of mankind (a word that included women) had found in the Virginia cigarette its supreme enjoyment.

"Between friends, intimacy is fostered by sharing the pleasure of smoking a cigar or pipe during friendship's intercourse, but a cigarette can make utter strangers to one another disposed to friendliness. The cigarette is a passport accepted by every country without a visa."

I don't know you from Adam, but seeing you're a smoker, let's strike up a friendship.' 'Lucky strike, eh ?' 'No, Gold Flake actually.'

Quiet Delight for Bertie Wooster's creator

Sir Compton Mackenzie - he was knighted in 1952 - had no stronger supporter in all this than P G Wodehouse (1881-1975), the famous creator of Jeeves, Bertie Wooster and PSmith, who was also honoured by Her Majesty with a knighthood - in 1975.

It could scarcely have escaped the notice of thinking men, he wrote in his autobiography *Over Seventy*, that the forces of darkness opposed to people like himself, who

liked a quiet smoke, were gathering momentum daily, and starting to throw their weight about more than somewhat.
From the fact that the American film actress Gloria Swanson stated that her disciples in her non-smoking campaign sent her flowers, Wodehouse imagined that she belonged to the school of thought that held that abstention from tobacco heightened the sense of smell.

> I don't want my sense of smell heightened. When I lived in New York I often found myself wishing that I didn't smell the place as well as I did.

'Gentlemen, you may twirl your fingers'

HE COULD NOT RECOMMEND Leo Tolstoy's suggestion for a smoking-substitute, that instead of lighting up you twirled your fingers. There rose before his mental eye the picture of some big public dinner (decorations will be worn) at the moment when the royal toast was being drunk.

> 'The Queen !'
> 'The Queen, God bless her !'
> 'Gentlemen, you may twirl your fingers.'

PLUM DID NOT THINK IT WOULD WORK. There would be a sense of something missing. But then, he said, what could you expect of a man who not only grew a long white beard, but declared that the reason people smoked was that they wanted to deaden their conscience ? To support this, Tolstoy instanced the case of a Russian murderer of Czarist times who, halfway through the assassination of his employer, found himself losing the old pep. 'I could not finish the job,' the desperado is quoted as saying, 'so I went from the bedroom into the dining room, sat down there and smoked a cigarette.' Only when he had 'stupefied himself with tobacco' commented Tolstoy, did he feel sufficiently fortified to return to the bedroom and complete his crime. See ?

To the Editor of THE TIMES

Smoke gets in the lights
From Dr J. J. Scott

Sir, For over 40 years I have happily completed your daily crosswords. Since giving up smoking cigars three months ago (voluntarily, but with a nudge from the Chancellor) I can hardly do half each day. I haven't completed more than half a dozen this year, not even the Saturday puzzles, for which one has more time. I have never been a rapid solver, and gone now are the joys of a two-cigar puzzle.

When I gave up cigarettes 20 years ago there were no such dire results. Can any ex-cigar-smoker reassure me that the sad effect is temporary?

I wonder how the entry would be affected if ever the venues for your annual competition were made non-smoking areas.

Yours faithfully,
JOHN SCOTT,
The Cottage, South
Rauceby,
Sleaford,
Lincolnshire,

Delayed Delight

Late Again ? Pleasure curtailed

The cross looks on the faces of these fuming passengers waiting on the platform for the 8.45 at 8.50 reflects their concern, not that they will be late in the office, but that they will not have time to complete The Times crossword, and finish their pipe, in the train before it reaches Victoria.

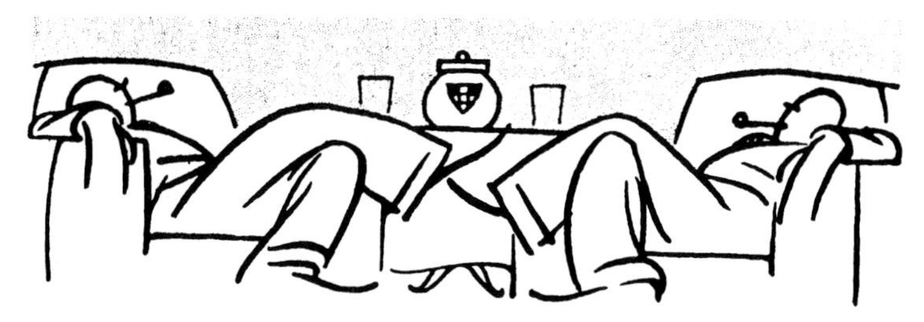

The Pipe of Tobacco

Why should life in sorrow be spent,
When pleasure points the road
Wherein each traveller with content
May throw off the ponderous load?

And instead, in ample measure,
Gather fruits too long left ripe;
What's this world without its pleasure?
What is pleasure but a pipe?

See the sailor's jovial state,
Mark the soldier's noble soul;
What doth heroes renovate?
What refines the splendid bowl?

Is it not tobacco dear,
That from the brow fell grief can wipe?
Yes! like them with jolly cheer,
I find pleasure in a pipe.

Some are fond of care and grief,
Some take pleasure in sad strife,
Some pursue a false belief -
Few there are that enjoy life.

Some delight in envy ever,
Others avaricious gripe;
Would you know our greatest pleasure?
'Tis a glowing social pipe.

From Pedlar's Pack of Ballads.

Uninterrupted Pleasure

REMEMBER MAIGRET ? Georges Simenon, the pipe-smoking creator of the pipe-smoking French detective played by pipe-smoking Rupert Davies in the British television series, makes sure that he does not have to interrupt his writing by having to fill another pipe.

June 1, 1951.

Georges Simenon
Shadow Rock Farm
Lakeville, Connecticut
Telephone Lakeville 749

Mr. Ralph Morrissey,
Book Review Editor,
The Nashville Tennessean,
Nashville, Tenn.

Dear Mr. Morrissey:

It's a pleasure to answer your very congenial letter. As a matter of fact, it's a pleasure to answer it at length, not that I think that all I will say may be of use in your article, but because your questions are not those that can be answered by yes or no, or again by an X in a square, as for a driving license.

The topic of pipes alone would require a whole chapter. I would guess by the way you broach it that you, yourself, are a pipe smoker.

I don't know if smoking helps me in my work nor in what is referred to as inspiration. Ever since the age of fifteen or sixteen, I have lighted a pipe upon arising in the morning and kept on smoking till bedtime. That means I have at least two pipes in my pocket at all times, and a dozen or so on my desk. It is quite true that I fill them all at once before I start my work so as not to be interrupted in the course of it.

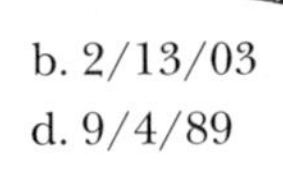

b. 2/13/03
d. 9/4/89

2

AN ISSUE? IN 1916 IT WAS A *Godsend*

Want to make an issue of it ?

Select any aspect of past behaviour which for years has been part of the landscape and has never changed its nature, choose to bring it into prominence and it can become an instant 'issue'. It is an impressive word meant to imply that if you are not worrying about it, you are NOT WITH IT, out of step with the march of progress. Think about it long enough, and you can convince yourself of the truth of what this chap is saying .

As Dr Richard Gordon points out in his *Alarming History of Medicine:*

What is health? 'A state of complete physical, mental and social well-being and not merely the absence of disease or infirmity,' defines the World Health Organisation. Which is unstatistical, but as helpful as asserting that happiness is achievable only in Heaven.

Oh dear ! Twhit-a-woo !
Can't be too careful - or can you ?

'Bad news - our new hair spray causes sterility if taken in massive doses by spotted owls.'

Adding a little spice to my life

I FIND IT A LITTLE RIDICULOUS that any reasonable person should have to waste time considering the problem of tobacco, a trivial matter in a world where we are threatened with annihilation from global catastrophes. There should be far more important things in the world to worry about than tobacco. Nobody recognises this more clearly than I do. I interpret the tobacco debate as a symptom of authoritarianism, and find it as essential to react against it as against any kind of manipulation, threat to human integrity or abrogation of individual freedom. I have smoked for more than fifty years and have never given the matter a thought - other than as a pleasant experience adding a little spice to my life. It has never been a problem for me, and I have no reason to believe that my smoking has been a problem for anybody else.

Dr Tage Voss,
Smoking and Common Sense, One Doctor's View, 1992

'I'm afraid Trevor's got a bit of a thing about smoking'

THE WIZARD OF ID

by Brant parker and Johnny hart

THE yelling, screaming, looking back in anger section

To the Editor of The Times

Osborne's delight goes up in smoke

From Mr John Osborne

Sir, For 40 years I have smoked various brands of Turkish cigarettes. Untipped, robust and fragrant, they always seemed to me the only cigarette tobacco worth smoking, and one of life's few and reliable pleasures.

I rarely smoked more than a packet a week. But puffing their exquisite fumes in the face of the army of prigs and bullies who dominate national life became an additional delight. Earlier this month, visiting Davidoff's in Jermyn Street for my regular stock-up, I discovered that I am no longer to indulge in this idle, satisfying sport because, so they tell me, a 'European' diktat forbids it.

I am perfectly prepared to believe that the issue is more complicated than this: nevertheless, to observe this nation falling over itself in frenzy to submit to such puny tyrannies, which extend to more fundamental principles like the legalities of personal freedom, choice and 'human rights' is dispiriting.

What baffles me about this craven abasement is that these directives are imposed upon us by a collective of countries united by one thing: their recent and superficial experience of democracy. Is raw memory also banished, along with unfiltered fags?

About half of these newly sprung nation states - Germany, Italy, France, Spain and Portugal - have been administered by regimes that were Nazi, fascist, communist, crypto-fascist for several decades during my own lifetime. These are now charged with the duty and power of inflicting their bloodily acquired standards of justice and respect for 'human rights' on those of my country and generation, who alone and deservedly opposed them all at terrible cost.

So soon, and after such a brief intermission, these successful and happily empowered heirs of Hitler, Mussolini, Himmler, Franco, Honecker, Salazar, Petain, Laval and the Greek colonels are to be enjoined to deprive me of the liberty and choice, even in the matter of what cigarettes I may be allowed to smoke.

The names of such men, who dictated the destinies of all these states, with the popular support or connivance of their people, are they forgotten so soon? Is no one permitted to ask; from whence comes such another?

As a schoolboy, I narrowly escaped from 'European' bombs on my doorstep. I can forgive this eagerness, but not the compounding of the insult by dashing the tobacco from my lips 40 years on.

Yours faithfully,
JOHN OSBORNE,
The Hurst, Clunton,
Craven Arms, Shropshire.

Cartoon Springfield News-Sun, Copley News Service

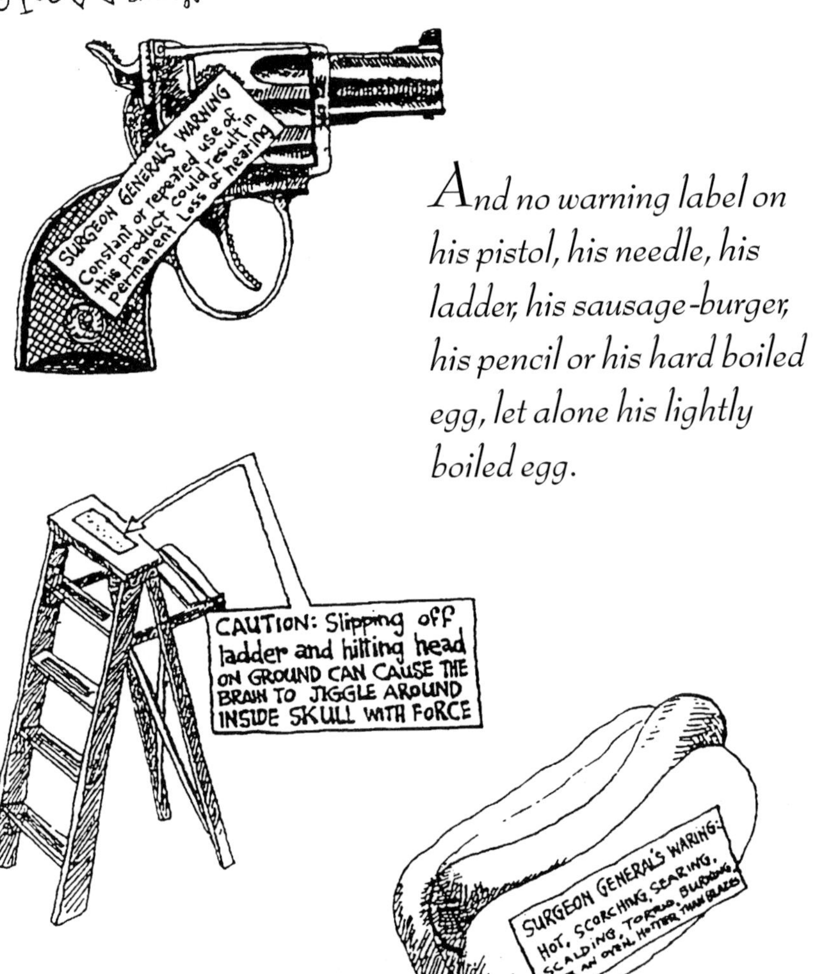

And no warning label on his pistol, his needle, his ladder, his sausage-burger, his pencil or his hard boiled egg, let alone his lightly boiled egg.

LEESCAPES BILL LEE
WAR, PESTILENCE, DESTRUCTION...
CRIME, FLOODS, FIRE...
RAIN, SLEET, SNOW...
CAUTION: THE SURGEON GENERAL HAS DETERMINED THAT EVENING NEWSCASTS MAY BE HAZARDOUS TO YOUR EMOTIONAL HEALTH.
©1982 Tribune Media Services, Inc. All Rights Reserved

GOOD IDEA... IT HAS BEEN SCIENTIFICALLY PROVEN THAT TOO MUCH POLITICS IS A HEALTH HAZARD!
NOW POLITICAL ADS BAN
SMOKES ADS OUT
IT HAS ITS DRAW BACKS!

Put that in your oven and don't cook it !

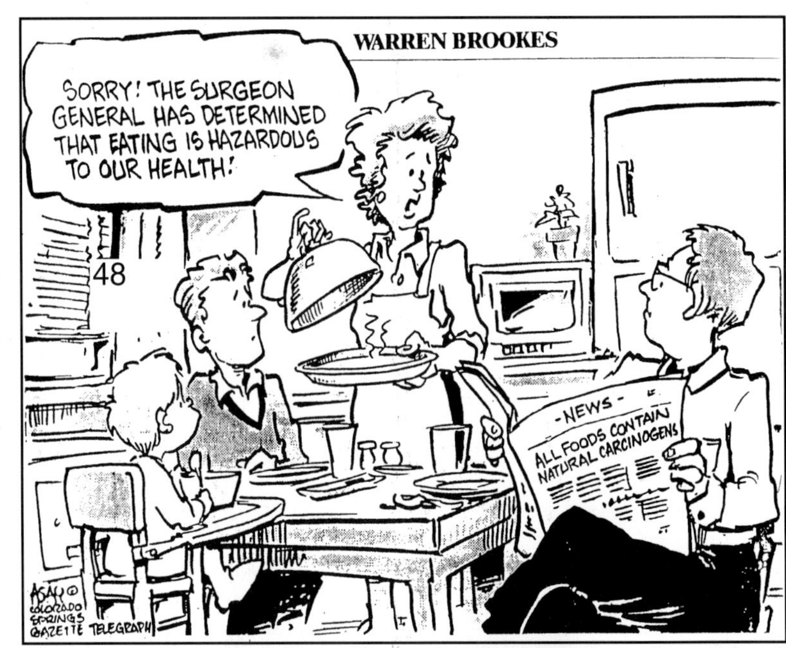

Reprinted by permission ofthe Colorado Springs Gazette Telegraph

THE POTTS by Jim Russell

See the POTTS in the SUN HERALD-in colour

WAY OF THE WORLD

AUBERON WAUGH

Smoking encouraged

IT WAS odd to read the new code for visitors to Antarctica, drawn up by the International Association of Antarctica Tour Operators. The Guidelines of Conduct include such instructions as these:

Do not walk on or otherwise damage the fragile plants such as lichens, mosses and grasses.

Do not smoke during shore excursions.

One tries to be reasonable about requests not to smoke indoors, but Antarctica covers about 5.5 million square miles with a population density of about one person per thousand square miles. Similarly, it seems strange that 'Keep Off the Grass' notices should arrive even before there are any humans there to walk on it.

The only interesting thing about Antarctica is how horribly inhospitable it is. Nobody could possibly wish to live there, and under those circumstances I don't see that it matters very much how its lichen, mosses and grasses fare.

The best possible use for it is as a gigantic tip to receive all the world's rubbish. Developed countries produce more rubbish than they can accommodate. Soon we shall start dumping it on each other, which is bound to cause trouble. Let the whole world decide to dump it on the South Pole.

And if those who visit the world's rubbish dump wish to smoke, for heaven's sake let them do so.

'Donald doesn't approve of smoking'

Tony Reeve

A Whiff of Overkill

Sir-Your simultaneous publication of articles on smoking and guns in America was intriguing.

I am left wondering whether that country, after giving up on real crime, has now dreamt up a fictitious one to put down as a sign of resolve and salve its conscience. Sometime soon a man will be acquitted when he pulls a gun to defend himself against someone threatening to light a cigarette in a building entered by ten or more people a week. But perhaps the lawyers will still be able to get him for the whiff of smoke emanating from his gun-barrel.

Damascus R Tamboezer

The Economist May 14th 1994

More than a *whiff*

What a lucky escape !

Who can deny its use Thoughtfully Taken ?

Cats may have had their goose
Cooked by tobacco-juice; *[1]
Still, why deny its use
  Thoughtfully taken ?
We're not as tabbies are.
Smith, take a fresh cigar !
Jones, the tobacco jar !
  Here's to thee, Bacon *[2]

C S Calverley *[3] 'Ode to Tobacco' in *Fly Leaves*

*[1] a lab experiment had just shown that two drops of nicotine on a cat's tongue killed it

*[2] This Bacon was a Cambridge tobacconist, not Francis.

*[3] Charles Stuart Calverley was the scholar, wit, versifier and parodist who dominated the youth of Cambridge University between 1869 and 1872.

PERISH THE THOUGHT that to-day's younger generation should know that **Britain's most famous steam railway builder was himself a puffer.**

STEAM PUFFER RAILWAY builder Isambard Kingdom Brunel was a thoughtful cigar puffer; and, what with having to work out the stresses and strains of the girders and rolled steel joists of all the viaducts, bridges and tunnels of his Great Western Railway, let alone coping with his own, it might be thought that no-one could have denied him the pleasure of a puff now and again, specially when posing for his photograph in front of the drag chains that controlled the launch down the slipway of the pioneering steam ship which he had had built at Bristol, the *Great Britain.*

THE GOVERNORS of the Isambard Brunel School at Portsmouth thought his indulgence would send the wrong message to their pupils if the great engineer was shown on their crest - horror of horrors ! - smoking a cigar.

Brunel cigar stubbed out

ANTI-SMOKERS have forced a school named after engineering genius Isambard Kingdom Brunel to remove the famous cigar from his mouth in its logo.

A spokeswoman for the Isambard Brunel Middle School in Portsmouth said his smoking image was now considered 'inappropriate' for children.

Daily Express
10th March 1994

No cheer from char

Issues come and issues go. Tea was once an 'issue'. If Brunel had had a cup of char in his hand instead of that cigar, doubtless many non-teadrinkers would have campaigned to have had it deleted for the school crest version of the photograph.

Tea ? The polite, afternoon, front parlour sitting-round-the-table brew-up that people today regard with affection as A Nice Cup of Tea, the cup that cheers ?
It was not always so regarded.

Vice of tea-drinking makes Englishmen less vigorous

SOME 200 YEARS AGO one Jonas Hanway ascribed the majority of feminine disorders to indulgence in tea-drinking. It was a vice, he said, which had lessened the vigour of Englishmen and deprived Englishwomen of beauty. It gave him the horrors to learn that no less than six ships and 500 seamen were being employed in this pernicious trade between China and England.

Reviewing Hanway's essay, Samuel Johnson, an admitted tea addict, had to admit, however, that tea was not fit for the lower classes, since it only gratified the taste without nourishing the body. Tea, he said, was 'a barren superfluity' proper only to amuse the idle, relax the studious and dilute the meals of those who cannot use exercise, and will not practise abstinence.

Out of favour, into favour, out of favour

Who can you believe ? A hundred years before that, the founder of Garraways Coffee House in the City of London was claiming that tea vanquished heavy dreams, eased the brain, strengthened the memory, made the body active and lusty, removed obstructions of the spleen, was good against lippitude distillations (sore eyes), removed lassitude, and purified adust (dusty) humours and a hot liver.

For good measure he insisted that tea was also good for colds, dropsies and scurvies.

He wouldn't give up *smoking* for all the tea in China

Tea never did him, her, you, the people next door, any harm ever *- except, as with everything else, in excess.*

As for tobacco, it would seem that Sir Walter Raleigh went a bit over the top when he requested that his coffin be lined with cigar boxes. But by the time he was in it with the lid on, the only after-effects he would suffer, if any, would be in the hereafter - where they were probably even more pleasurable than while swashbuckling round the Spanish Main.

They must be choking !

The custom of Venezuelan Indians, on the other hand, to smoke cigars backwards so as not to waste smoke, could not have affected them other than then and there.

And if they didn't think that was excessive, then, whatever effect it had, served them right - a right good do.

IN **1916** IT WAS A GODSEND

ARE THE CIGARETTES APPRECIATED?

The editor of *B.A.T. Bulletin* asked the tommies

SERGEANT WAKEFIELD:- 'They come as a godsend to us out here.'

PRIVATE H. H. FODEN:- 'Tommy loves Woodbines more than his grub.'

MR. A. E. WILLIAMS:- 'The famous Gold Flake are great favourites with the French.'

SIGNALLER BRYANT:- 'I need not repeat how welcome these gifts are out here.'

PRIVATE LEWIS, in hospital, Malta:- 'They came just at the right time, as smoking is about the only thing I am capable of now.'

SIGNALLER C. T. BRYANT:- 'The boys have been smoking "my health" and that of "my firm" this morning in "Gold Flake" - a luxury most of us have not tasted since July last.'

BOMBARDIER SYMONS:- 'The B.A.T. has quite an honoured name in our Battery, and the Cigarettes I have had have been worth their weight in gold to our chaps.'

LIEUTENANT GARDNER:- 'During my leave a parcel of Gold Flake and Capstan Tobacco arrived for me, and the well known green label was recognised in the Mess and on my return I found they had all been smoking my health.'

PRIVATE A. L. DRURY:- 'They came at the right moment, when I was reduced to smoking "ration" cigarettes of unknown origin.'

The Point of View

'Well, if it don't get merrier than this by Christmas, it won't be up to much'

Sleepy Feeling of Contentment

How it feels to be on leave.

Old soldiers found smoking more like eating. The effect seemed so distinct as to be felt in the pit of the stomach. A sleepy feeling of contentment countered cold, damp and fatigue. After a few puffs a man could endure more - or thought he could. Perhaps, since tobacco was the only indulgence a man could take with him in the front line to assure himself of his individuality, it tranquillized the more. Perhaps it was the most complex alternative focus of attention and thus allowed overwhelming danger to be atomized most satisfactorily. Soldiers without cigarettes in this century are the difference between Hollywood films and newsreel actuality

from Dennis Winter *Death's Men*

THE SUB-LIEUTENANT.

Only the Colonel rated a cigarette holder.

THE COLONEL.

The cigarettes which large numbers of Other Ranks puffed were given them by WOODBINE WILLIE

Rev. Geoffrey Studdert Kennedy (Woodbine Willie) 1885-1929

This was Geoffrey A Studdert Kennedy MC, the First World War army chaplain described on his memorial tablet in Worcester Cathedral, placed there after he died in 1929, as 'a poet, a prophet, a passionate seeker after truth, an ardent advocate of Christian fellowship'.

Small with bat ears, large brown eyes and generally untidily dressed, he spoke in a broad Irish brogue and could swear like a trooper. In January 1916 he was posted to the Base at Rouen where the troops waited, for the most part in the canteen by the railway sidings, before climbing on to the train that took them to the Front.

They spent less than a day there. S-K would go to the piano and sing. He then held a short service.

As Sir John Smyth writes in his Story of the Army Chaplains, *In This Sign Conquer:*

> They were nearly all very homesick, and showed him their family photographs. They gave him their letters to post. When the time came for them to entrain, S-K went down the train distributing his Woodbine cigarettes until he was left alone, waving to them from the platform. Hence his nickname - *Woodbine Willie.*

Cigarette tin breastplate saved Watkins's life

Mr. Robson has forwarded to us a Respirator and Capstan Cigarette Tin, presented by Sapper E. Watkins of the Royal Engineers, and mentioned in our issue of October 23rd. It will be remembered that while engaged upon night work in the Dardanelles, Watkins was struck by a bullet, which, entering his haversack upon his back, struck the tin, thereby being deflected, causing it to pass out through the side of the haversack, thus saving his life, or at any rate from being wounded. The Directors were very interested in the tin, and it now reposes in our Museum, which is assuming large proportions. Poor Watkins, it may be recollected, had his leg amputated as a result of a shrapnel wound, so he must be regarded as decidely unlucky after his first escape. *B.A.T. Bulletin* 1916.

Don't light three cigarettes with one match - a 'superstition' or . . . ?

An explanation of the origin of the superstition which considers the lighting of three cigarettes with one match to be dangerous has at last been made.

'You see it was this way,' says James Valentine, Jr., the official explainer in Jersey State, U.S.A. 'The superstition originated with the British army in the Boer War. The sniping ability of the Boer sharp-shooters was of a high order, most of them having been born and brought up in the wilds where all sorts of shooting was second nature to them. The British Army soon learned that when lighting a smoke at night if the match was held long enough for three men to light from it it was also just long enough to enable an alert sniper to draw a bead on the match flame, with the result that the last man was frequently killed. And so in this way arose the belief that it was "unhealthy" to light three cigarettes on a match. This belief grew into a superstition which was handed down through the British Army, and they brought it with them into the last war.' *B.A.T. Bulletin.* November, 1921

A CASTLE IN THE AIR

'A few more, Bert, and that there chateau won't be worth livin' in.'

WE HOPE YOU GET YOUR CIGARETTES!

LANCE-CORPORAL F. A. RICE, TO MR. ROBSON:- 'Ever so many thanks for sending the Gold Flake cigarettes, which reached me quite safely, but, owing to my being detached from the Battalion for the last month, and just having returned, I have only just got them, as I left instructions not to forward any parcels.

My battalion have just gone into the trenches again, after a month's rest, so I shall have to go up to rejoin them there to-morrow. Will you kindly deduct from my salary for the cigarettes and hand the balance to the Bulletin, as I think it about time another subscription was due from me.'

Published in honour of the Staff of the BRITISH-AMERICAN TOBACCO COMPANY, LIMITED, who have joined His Majesty's Forces.

THE *power* OF A *cigarette*

'Tis Yuletide out in the trenches,
The night it is cold and drear,
With never a sign
From our sturdy line,
Of the foeman who lurks so near.

Our boys they are staunch and ready,
Though chilled to the bone - and wet,
But their eyes grow bright
As they place a light
To a B.A.T. cigarette.

Merely a pinch of tobacco
Encased in a paper shell,
But it has a pow'r
In the midnight hour
The soldier alone can tell.

For it whispers of dear old England;
Of Home – and his heart's desire,
And it seems to show
In its ruddy glow
The gleam of the homestead fire.

It brings to his mental vision
The faces of those he loves,
And he softly sighs
As he clasps his eyes
In his tattered and war worn gloves.

It speaks to him, too, of friendship,
And colleagues who ne'er forget,
And his heart grows glad
As the soldier lad
Inhales from his cigarette.

'Tis Yuletide out in the trenches,
The enemy close at hand,
But he quite forgets
While his cigarettes
Whisper softly of 'Motherland.'

Dec. 25th 1915. *B.A.T. Bulletin*

'Heard the latest rumour up from the back, George? War's going to be over next week.'

'Ho. Well, I hope it don't upset my going on leave next Tuesday.'

'CARRIED OFF.'

THE CLEVER SKETCH reproduced this week is one of Mr. J. Milton's. We quote below a part of his letter:-

'I enclose sketch of self being carried off the battlefield. The fact that the rear stretcher-bearer has insinuated himself into the stretcher, so to speak, is due to shortage of paper on my part, and no blame, therefore, attaches to the portly old sport himself. He regaled me, during the journey, with anecdotes of his home life, of the pleasures and trials of thirty years' connubiality, "but," he said, "my wife has always regarded me as more of a friend than a husband." '

B.A.T. Bulletin, 1916

A buttress to morale and tension-reliever in World War II as well

In the Second World War of 1939-1945 Woodbines were still the favourites, along with Players and Gold Flake. When American troops came to Britain they insisted on smoking only the brands they were used to back home - Chesterfield, Lucky Strike, Camel. In *World War II: The Sharp End*, John Ellis tells how they left many thousands of cartons of obscure brands to rot on the shelves of the PX, which were bought from the US Quartermaster before they became unsmokable, however, by the Canadian and Australian governments for their less fastidious servicemen. Ten million packets of them!

Though cigarettes were theoretically non-essential, the various high commands were sensible of the need to give them a high priority. Many of the men called up had been smokers in civilian life and the effort of trying to stop would have been a severe psychological strain which added to the other tensions of the front line. There cigarettes were a vital buttress to morale and the most stringent black-out regulations could not prevent men from lighting up.

THE PLEASURE WAS IN THE PUFFING - ANYTHING

IT WAS THE LIGHTING UP and puffing the smoke - of *anything* - that was the attraction for many. Writing in the Players' house magazine *Navy Cuttings*, one J A Rhodes told how he was captured in North Africa and sent to a Prisoner of War camp in Italy. He was there for seven months before the first parcel of 'comforts' arrived. 'My mates and I were so desperate for a cigarette that we even rolled raspberry leaves which our captors used to make tea, into pieces of notepaper or newspaper, and smoke these.'

J A Taylor, another Players' employee, was arrested by the Japanese on a rubber estate in British North Borneo in 1942 and interned in a POW camp in Sarawak for three and a half years. 'Throughout all this period we all smoked the unfermented native tobacco known as "hay", which it closely resembled, and was sold to us at ever-increasing and fantastic prices by the Japanese. We also smoked the leaves of the paw-paw tree, egg plant and even dried tea leaves.

Some prefer it herbal

Fifty years later Michael Butler, its editor, was writing in the Pipesmokers Guide of 1993:

Our mail-bag has included several letters asking about the possibility of adding herbs to regular pipe tobacco. One such query came from a pipesmoker in his 20's, Jonathan St John of Swansea. (Suppressing my prejudices about herbal remedies) I asked Dr Isidore Redstone, whose family introduced Balkan Sobranie to Britain and who is now a director of Honeyrose Products of Stowmarket who make and distribute herbal products, if this was a practicable idea.

I R: I think there is always a minority of smokers who like to experiment. I would suggest one part of marshmallow and one part of an equal mixture of angelica, lavender and hyssop could be mixed in a ratio of 1:1 with ready rubbed tobacco - not the aromatic brands because the flavour of the herbs wouldn't come through.

Editor: What are the other herbs used and what are their qualities?

I R: There are a lot of commonly used herbs. They are normally smoked having been sun-dried, either on their own or in mixtures which can be matured in honey, wine, fruit juices, etc. Here are some: Angelica root - sweet, aromatic. Aniseed - distinctive, aromatic. Birch leaf - neutral. Californian poppy - relaxing. Chamomile flowers - neutral. Coltsfoot leaf - characteristic aroma. Damiana leaf - distinctive, mild aphrodisiac. Eyebright - distinctive aroma. Ginseng leaf - strong, characteristic taste. Gutu kola - mild stimulant. Hops - distinctive, mild relaxant. Lemon balm - sweet. Liquorice - distinctive. Lobelia leaf - 'indian tobacco'. Meadowsweet - sweet. Raspberry leaf - fruity, mild stimulant. Rose petal - delicate fragrance. Spearmint - menthol flavour. Thyme - aromatic, sweet.

3

PASSIVE PROTEST - ACTIVE *Preference*

It's not his puffing
I find put-uffing;
It's just so sordid
That he (and not I)
can affordid.

Silent Protest

Eyeball-to-Eyeball Protest

"If you wanted the no-smoking section, you should have said so".
Drawing by Dedini; © 1993
The New Yorker Magazine, Inc

Passive Protest

Whose idea was it to come here anyway?

Active protest

Reeve

The Considerate Protester

"Does that satisfy you?"

No Compromise Protester

"All right, all *right!* Keep your hair on!
I only said that **maybe** – *maybe* – next time
you try something a bit milder. No need to
blow your top!
Oh, you have. Oh well."

AUBERON WAUGH

Who pays the nanny?

DESPITE the deliberate twisting of statistics in a contrary sense, the fact is well known to those who investigate the matter that passive smoking is one of the cheapest and least dangerous pleasures available to modern man.

Why, then, does the Department of the Environment issue a 'code of practice' urging owners and managers of banks, post offices, hospitals, schools and other buildings which people have to visit to ban smoking altogether? Why does it urge that in restaurants, hotels, pubs, theatres and other dwellings visited by people out of choice, no smoking should be the general practice, with smoking limited to special areas?

If any of this bossy nonsense were enacted, one out of three adults in this country would be seriously inconvenienced and annoyed. That is about 14 million voters, although few, I fancy, would bother to write and warn the Government in advance.

Instead, the Government is in daily communication with such pressure groups as Ash. In fact, these groups are about the only sections of the public with whom ministers have any contact at all, in their vital business of making decisions and feeling important. Nobody else is prepared to waste time talking to politicians.

In the case of Ash, which tells me it has 'about 1,000 supporters', there would be no pressure group at all if the Government did not support it out of public funds. Effectively, the Government uses public money to create and support groups to pressurise it, because it is terrified it will otherwise be ignored. I hope all smokers will immediately desert whichever bank first declares itself a smoke-free zone.

Daily Telegraph, 1991

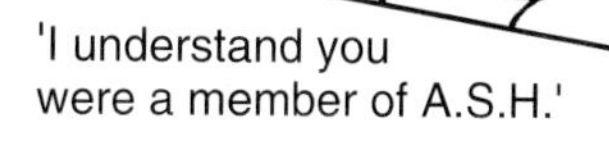

'I understand you were a member of A.S.H.'

MATT *gives up smoking*

INTERNATIONAL HERALD TRIBUNE

THE BOSTON SUNDAY GLOBE

'Don't get excited, lady, I'm smoking oat bran.'

'Passive Smoking' Without Tears

This picture explained

This woman is not smoking. Her look is conveying to the man on her left, who is the subject of an exercise in pipe-smoking - a subjective pipe-smoker, right? - that she objects to being subjected to having, willy-nilly, to whiff whatever it is he is burning in his pipe, and that she fears the irritation it will give her. To call her a 'passive smoker' makes it look as if she is going through the same exercise as he is, only involuntarily. She is not. In this case, on hearing that he is smoking porridge, her fears, based on what she has read in the newspapers, are allayed.

She is not talking, he is. Being a simple wayfarer on a simple train journey he would fear for his sanity if he heard himself calling her a passive talker.

'. . . apparently he's a passive anti-passive smoking activist . . .'

Passive Moustache Tickling

Active Moustache Singeing

This ancestor of the above was concerned, not with the good or bad effect which his smoking might have on his adored one, but on his moustache, which, it upset him to think, thereby ran the risk of being singed.

Conceited cad !

'Don't be daft. It's the only place in the building where he can have a smoke.'

'Well if you're a passive smoker why don't you shut up and be passive then?'

WAY OF THE WORLD

AUBERON WAUGH

Another danger

ON THURSDAY I took the Scottish Pullman from King's Cross and found all the first-class seats occupied by crowds of people who had read that morning about the new chocolate-flavoured potato crisps available in Scotland and Newcastle upon Tyne. They were travelling up to sample them.

Alas, I had to get out at York, and so cannot report on the taste or texture of this new delight. No doubt somebody will soon tell us they are bad for us, but the health fanatics have to be quick off the mark nowadays with all these exciting new foods.

I was pleased to learn that the American government has decided margarine is every bit as bad for the heart as butter. I hope it bans the consumption of margarine on all public transport, just as National Express has banned all smoking on its coaches.

National Express is being particularly sadistic in this, because its services are used, more than anything else, by students and the poor, who tend to be committed and enthusiastic smokers.

Although no connection has ever been established between passive smoking and any of the graver illnesses attributed to primary smoking - cancer, emphysema, etc - the dangers of passive margarine consumption have scarcely been investigated at all. It is a terrifying thought that if you sit next or opposite to or immediately in front of a margarine eater in a train, bus or aeroplane, you may be absorbing the substance from the margarine eater's breath not only in your throat and lungs but even through your skin.

Daily Telegraph 1992

Passive Musicians

Keep your distance

If you want to smoke, sir, you'll have to walk on the other side of the street.'

WAY OF THE WORLD

AUBERON WAUGH

Passive litigation

IF I were a ratepayer of Stockport Metropolitan Borough I think I might feel a little resentful to see ú15,000 of my money given away to a local government officer who claimed she had suffered illness and inconvenience as a result of colleagues' smoking. I would have liked to have seen the laryngitis, painful glands, permanent runny nose and bronchitis - from which she claimed to have suffered for several years - tested in court and severally costed.

Passive smoking does not cause obesity, but gross obesity can easily give rise to breathing difficulties. Passive smoking does not cause bacterial infections, which is what laryngitis and bronchitis frequently are. If Miss Bland was nursing bacteria, any colleagues who caught an infection might reasonably sue her - or sue the council for allowing her in the same room.

The council decided not to defend the action, acting on insurers' advice, and anyone with experience of the gigantic racket of civil law will understand why.

Perhaps it is only the incompetence and ancient crooked ways of our legal profession which prevent us collapsing into the American model, where everyone sues for a sneeze.

Daily Telegraph 1993

Mathys Dre, Kuringen

Pacific Island Passivity

'I can't think how it got there; there was no mention of it in the Lunn Poly brochure.' What a whiff ! Can't think why they're frowning. Absolutely wizard !

Aromatic vapour whiffing by preference

As an alternative to getting the pleasure of tobacco smoke direct from a cigarette, cigar or pipe in their mouth, some people choose to get it second-hand, as it were, from apparatus which automatically puffs smoke out into the room which they then whiff for all they are worth. 'Apparatus', that is, dolled up as an automaton doll like this one from France, of a gent in a curly brimmed top hat with smoke billowing out from underneath his drooping moustache, and holding a cigarette in a holder to the mouth of his French poodle; or (*right*) a nattily dressed negro.

Neger-Raucherautomat vermutlich J. Phalibois, Paris

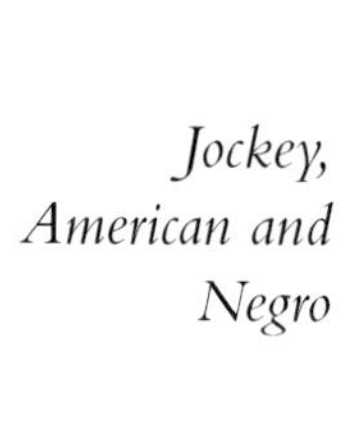

Jockey, American and Negro

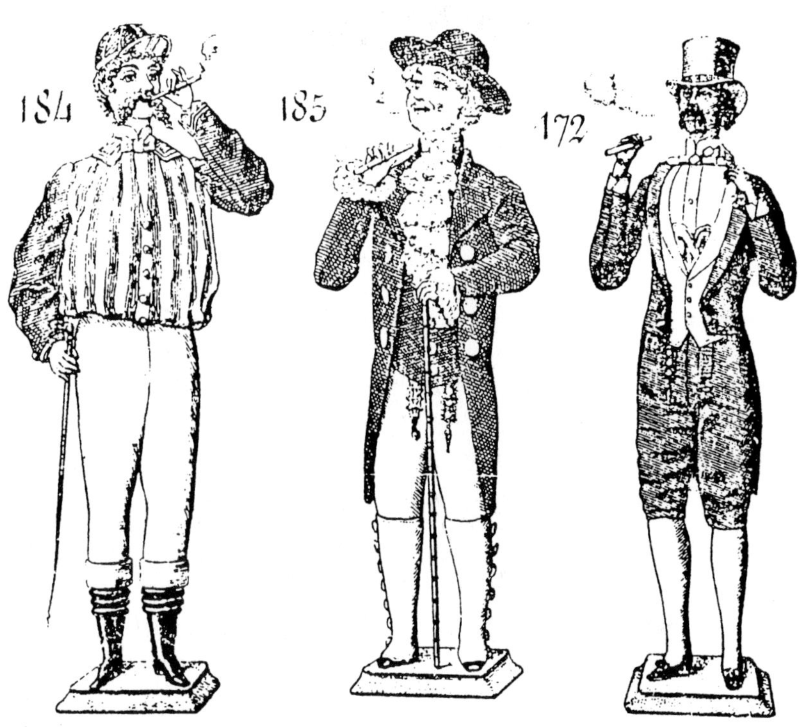

Here are three more French automaton smoking figures from the 1870s catalogue of Decamps and Lambert, all in brightly coloured satin suits; and on the left some of the 'oriental' china dolls in Bestelmeier's catalogue from Germany.

How did they work ?

The 'smoke' came from smouldering aromatic pastils placed in the body of the doll which rose and escaped through the only hole, the figure's mouth. The French Jockey, American and Negro had mechanisms that moved their eyes and mouths, turned their heads and raised their arms. The china dolls were static.

Pastil-burning was widespread in Britain a hundred years ago. One Charles Lillie, a London perfumer, had a contract to burn pastils each morning in the Houses of Parliament before the start of business. They were a paste of honey-water, benzoin, sealing wax and gum arabic in rose water and spirit of musk.

Up the jib, up the nose

Anyone who wanted a less public way of whiffing aromatic vapours could press his nose to a perfumed glove. No fear of being called effeminate. The macho military leader Napoleon Bonaparte was a perfume glove addict. He ordered 24 pairs of them for his own use only weeks before the Battle of Waterloo. The kings and nobles of France would don gloves of soft leather impregnated with ambergris or musk. There was a craze too for whiffing aromatic vapours from the perfumed sails of ships. Up with the scented spinnaker, up the jib, up the nose !

What a whiff from this lot !

4

MAKES THE WHOLE WORLD

Common ground

Smoking makes the whole world chummy. It breaks down social barriers, common ground for highflyer and down-and-out, for people of different ages, different races, different genders, who worship different gods.

When two smokers meet, no matter their age, sex, race or religion, their faces break into a smile - see the grins on the faces of the two old codgers above.

Hands across the sea ? For John Haloftis of Greece it is Pipes Across the Sea, and in April 1994 he told Peter Wiseman who runs the international Pipe Club of London, why.

The feeling which he has for his pipes is, he believes, the same the world over.

He has 515 PIPES to choose from

'I BELIEVE,' Colonel Haloftis told Peter Wiseman, 'that we pipe-smokers are much closer than any other people with a common occupation in international level. We are in a way the most internationalised persons with the greatest number of common habits, attitudes and feelings. You see it is not that we care about one certain item only; we feel the same way about so many details in our pipe loving. It is the little things, the little joys we can afford in this life that make us happy. With us it is continuous from the moment we choose the pipe for the day.'

If he smokes a different pipe each day, having 515 of them means it will be a rare occasion when he smokes any of them more than once - but a delightful one.

THE LITERARY DUSTMAN

He gets the same enjoyment from the same cigar

A man who has risen in the world through his 'lib'ral hedication', without however claiming to hold the lofty station of some folks, the Literary Dustman, seen lounging in his over-furnished front parlour, grinning and bearing the excruciating sounds coming from the direction of the piano, is at one with the colonel of another nationality and another era in finding pleasure in smoking - as he points out in his own poetical composition:

We dines at four and arter that
I smokes a mild Awanna,
Or gives a lesson to the lad
Upon the grand pianna.

Puff smoke into another's face and they all puffed at yours

YOU CAN'T TELL YARNS to yourself. You can, but you've heard them all before. There's got to be a roomful of you, and you've got to be in the right mood. Smoking has been putting people in the right mood for donkey's years, and you know how long that is. Not only for spinning yarns but listening to the spinner and even (occasionally) laughing at his jokes.

When casual acquaintances found they got on with one another and liked the smell of their tobacco, they met by arrangement not chance; the informal circle became A Club - and a pretty well-regularised one if the rules which Mr Twig insisted on enforcing for this eighteenth-century Smoaking Club is anything to go by.

THE SMOAKING CLUB.

The framed notice on the right of the print reads as follows:

'RULES

1st. *No Gemman to be a member of this Society who cannot smoke three pipes at one sitting.* N.B. *No spitting.*

2nd. *No member's pipe to be more than 14 inches nor less than nine unless permitted so to do by the Landlady.*

3rd. *Every member to find his own stopper.*

4th. *Any member who puffs designedly in the face of another to be fined sixpence or be puffed at in return by the whole company.*

5th. *All fines to be spent in porter.*

T. Twig, Secy.'

A 'Gemman' of course was a Gentleman; 'porter' was a dark brown bitter beer.

Offensive and insulting

PUFFING SMOKE INTO A PERSON'S FACE was regarded as an impudent, offensive, insulting act, a mild form of slapping him across the chops, almost a declaration of war.

Two hundred years ago cartoonists were fond of depicting the House of Commons as a Smoking Club whose ill-mannered members spent their time quarrelling and insulting each other by puffing tobacco smoke into each other's faces - like Thomas Gillray's cartoon of 1793 (*left*), drawn at a time when England was about to start a prolonged war with France led by its dictator Bonaparte.

That's the Speaker on the left, and on either side of him the Prime Minister and the Leader of the Opposition.

Here we go again !

A hundred and fifty years after Gillray, in 1944 cartoonist Low was showing another gathering of smokers round a table who had met to settle the future of Europe, threatened by an even more disruptive dictator called Adolf Hitler.

Ah! Mon Cher General! Where have you been all this time?

Conviviality's the name of the game

CHURCHWARDEN SOCIETIES were organised on a more formal basis. They were dining clubs which met about six times a year and had an even more elaborate set of rules. But conviviality was the name of the game. Every session ended with the whole company lighting up clay 'churchwarden' pipes, like the one historian Thomas Carlyle is smoking here. He's consoling himself after his fanatically tidy-minded housekeeper swept his manuscript of his history of the French Revolution off his desk and threw it on the fire, which meant he had to start all over again.

Why 'Churchwarden'?

THE PARSON GAVE HIS SERMON at the end of the service, and it was the Done Thing for the churchwarden on duty that Sunday to settle down in his box pew at the back of the church, fill his long clay pipe with tobacco, light it and puff away to allay the tedium of hearing for the umpteenth time how, if he was to avoid the torments of hellfire, he would have radically to change his lifestyle. The long clay pipe became associated in the public mind with this pillar of Anglican society, and this design of pipe became known as a Churchwarden.

Old Holborn - where smokers clubbed together

IN 1885 A LADIES SMOKING CLUB was formed, which met in Staple Inn, Holborn. How long this lasted is uncertain, but The Smokers Club of 14 male members which was formed in 1906, also in Holborn, carried on until the Georgian house near Gray's Inn Pump in which they met was destroyed in the Blitz of 1941.

The Smokers Club was the idea of a group of friends who would gather for a smoke and a yarn in the somewhat cramped parlour of the Eagle Tavern. When bachelor solicitor Ernest Stubbs heard they were looking for a larger place in which to meet, he suggested they used as a Club Room the spacious oak-pannelled room in his house overlooking the Benchers' Garden of Gray's Inn.

Gems of Delicacy

STUBBS ARRANGED for the married couple who were his housekeepers to run The Smokers Club, Mr Busby and Madame Busby - she was of foreign descent. Mister Busby was secretary, treasurer and steward, and his wife 'hostess'. Madame B, though a non-smoker, made up for the fact by being a gifted musician. When not quietly knitting in a corner and, when she had something to contribute, entering into the conversation, she entertained the company with 'gems of delicacy' on the pianoforte.

Today's Churchwarden Societies

Several Churchwarden Societies, modelled on the eighteenth-century originals have been formed in recent times by 'dedicated gentlemen' like the Mercians who in the 1990s meet in The Rising Sun at Willington near Derby, and hold joint meetings with other Churchwarden Societies such as those at Aylesbury and Tavistock.

Macnab rounds up 100 pipe clubs

Not bagpipes, stupid !
It was more than a hundred local tobacco pipe clubs which in 1969 another bachelor Peter Macnab brought together under the banner of The Pipe Club of Great Britain. Most members of such clubs worked in the tobacco trade, and Macnab's PCGB was strongly backed by a number of manufacturers and retailers. A minority were their customers.

Wiseman joins the new one in London

One of the largest of the local groups brought into the PCGB's fold was The Pipe Club of London. 'At the inaugural meeting in 1969,' remembers Peter Wiseman, now its honorary secretary and treasurer, 'I was one of approximately 20 non-trade "civilians" out of a total of around 45 founder members.'

When ill-health forced Peter Macnab to resign as director, and no-one could be found to take his place, the Pipe Club of Great Britain fell apart. Central funding ceased and member clubs had to fend for themselves.

The Pipe Club of London Goes International

Most local clubs found it impossible to continue but, thanks to the help they received from John Brumfit and Radford Tobacco Ltd, The Pipe Club of London not only survived but went international. This stemmed from Peter Wiseman and his colleagues allowing Brumfit and Radford's German subsidiary Alois Pöschl GmbH to market their tobacco in tins marked 'Approved by Members of the Pipe Club of London, England'.

'I take it he's one of our provincial members?'

Promoting good fellowship

As a result more than half the membership of The Pipe Club of London in 1994 are German-speaking, some 189 of them. Eighty-five of them are British, 15 come from Italy, 13 from the United States and 11 each from Belgium and Spain. Others come from all over the world. A few may be collectors of pipes but the Club is primarily for pipe *smokers*; only few members have any connection with the trade. Its prime object is to promote good fellowship among members from wherever they hail. They meet once a month in Marylebone and publish a journal. A regular fixture in their calendar is a darts match against members of The Handlebar Club described as 'an organisation for those who sport their facial hair with pride' and nothing to do with that →

Peter Wiseman keeps abreast of what is going on in the pipe-smoking world on the other side of the Atlantic through the columns of Tom Dunn's remarkable publication *The Pipe Smoker's Ephemeris*, and the activities reported in it of the Coterians, as Dunn calls members of his Universal Coterie of Pipe Smokers, based in New York.

He burnt his handlebar

MEMBERS MAY HAVE been able to throw a nifty dart when challenged by the likes of Jimmy Edwardes and other moustachioed whisker-twirlers, but what separates the men from the boys among members of a smoking club is the competition which showed who could 'make smoke' - from a pipe or a cigar - the longest without going out.

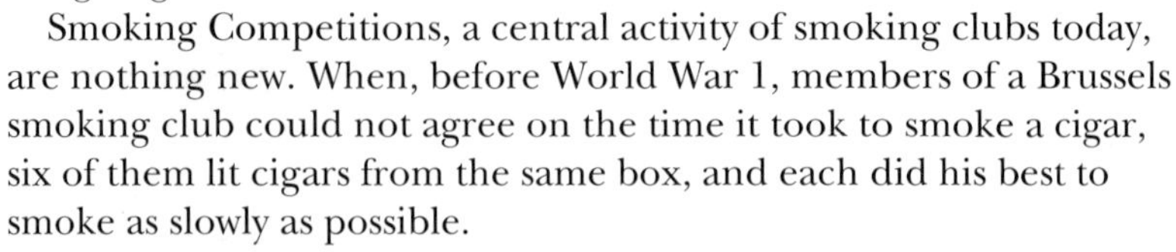

Smoking Competitions, a central activity of smoking clubs today, are nothing new. When, before World War 1, members of a Brussels smoking club could not agree on the time it took to smoke a cigar, six of them lit cigars from the same box, and each did his best to smoke as slowly as possible.

Five had finished after one and three-quarters of an hour. One of them could have gone on much longer, only he set fire to his moustache, and saw the wisdom of throwing in the towel - or applying a wet one to his upper lip to contain the conflagration. The sixth contestant was the victor by keeping his cigar going for two hours and 50 minutes.

Tobacco leaf in place of tea leaves

MANY YEARS AGO two men from Oundle decided which of them was the more accomplished smoker by seeing, in a private competition, which of them could keep two ounces of tobacco smoking the longest, which each of them lit *inside a teapot.*

At the word Go! each put his mouth to the spout and drew for all they were worth. When, after not so long, one of them gave up, the other declared himself the winner - but he too was unable to continue until the whole two-ounce fill in the teapot was fully burnt.

In 1723 the challenge concerned a larger bowl-ful. In that year, in an Oxford theatre, a smoking competition was held, the winner of which would be 'any one (man or woman) that could smoak out three ounces of tobacco first without drinking or going off the stage'. The prize was twelve shillings. A journeyman tailor looked like winning, but, said a contemporary report, 'an old man that had been a soldier, and smoaked gently, came off the conqueror, smoaking the three ounces quite out.'

Good sport

Did anyone think of giving twelve shillings, not to the man (or woman) who kept his (or her) pipe going the longest, but sported the longest pipe ?

Maybe.

Our illustration, only recently discovered in a nineteenth-century workbasket in Surbiton (sorry, Thames Ditton), shows a not-very-sure-of-himself competition judge saying to himself 'I think I'll give the prize for the longest pipe to this fellow'; while his Other Self (reflected in the mirror - got it?) says 'But what about those two characters down below ?'

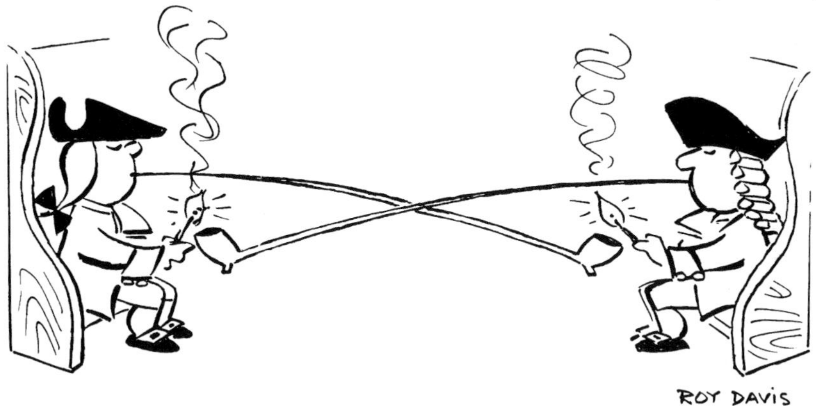

Not in the (longest) pipe line ?

Just precisely how this Longest Pipe Competition worked out is not revealed. But it is known that when the bearded man in the tile hat left the room with the fireplace (without actually measuring the length of the pipe of the man in the pointed shoes), he encountered the Smoking Hussar, and could tell, without the help of a tape measure, that his pipe, though long, was shorter than the civvy's, and he could award him second prize.

But perhaps he hadn't entered for the competition and was just wiling away the time before the next battle having a cup of coffee ?

Exit competition judge, stroking his beard, even more unsure of himself than ever before.

Smoking hussar, about 1800.

Doesn't ring true

An unlikely story is the one about this picture of two gents, one of whom has misread the competition rules. 'No no!' it is said his friend is saying, 'it's for the best smoke rings not funnels.' Whether, after all that blowing the wrong shape, they came to blows of another sort is not recorded. But, as everyone knows, the art is to blow separated smoke rings, each a perfect circle, which keep their shape for at least a minute. Right ?

THE MOST REMARKABLE PIPE IN THE WHOLE KINGDOM

In 1973 The Briar Pipe Trade Association and The Pipe Club of Great Britain held a competition, not for the longest pipe in the UK but 'the most remarkable'. It was a term interpreted as indicating rarity or originality in design, craftmanship and engineering. It could be any size, but if it was too large to fit into the owner's pocket he had to be able to transport it by whatever means he chose - lower it by helicopter ? - to Dunhills in London's Jermyn Street where the judging was to take place. If it was obviously too unwieldy an affair to get into the lift to take up to the boardroom where the judges were assembled, they condescended to descend to the ground floor and inspect it there.

Carburettor from the Heart of England

IT WAS UP TO THE OWNER to demonstrate, by himself lighting it up and making smoke, that his contraption was smokable - or assembling his team for an orchestrated drawing-off of smoke from a multi-stemmed model.

Materials of pipes entered in 1973 ranged from the claw of a crab to horse-shoe nails. The winning pipe was made from the carburettor of a 1933 Riley Ascot, the creation of Brian Cole of the Heart of England Pipe Club of Coventry.

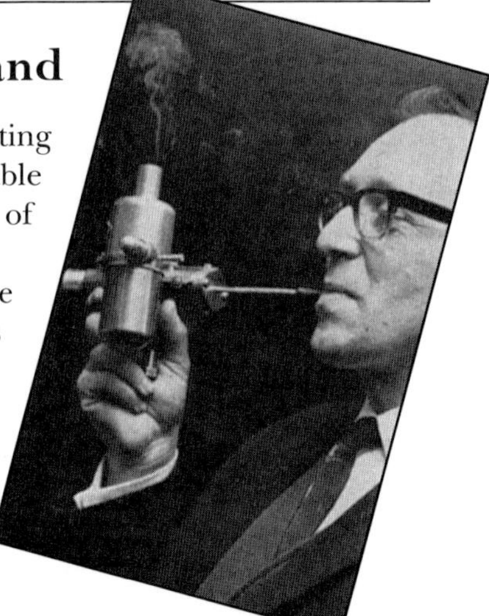

Brian Cole with his winning 1973 entry

National Pipesmoking Championship

For a number of years Imperial Tobacco Ltd, the successors to Ogden, England, under the St Bruno label, sponsored a National Pipesmoking Competition. Each club held its own heat, the winner of which received a pipe of his choice and ten pounds. Some 120 heat winners took part in the national competition in London, the champion receiving a cheque for £1,000.

Guide lines for holding these competitions were drawn up by the Pipe Club of Great Britain based on the experience of international competitions throughout the world. The winner of the competition is the one who smokes the longest without relighting.

No poking & probing the tobacco, but you can tamper with it (in a sense) - blow me down !

The only tool permitted in a pipe smoking competition, state the guide lines drawn up by the Pipe Club of Great Britain, based on international experience, is a tobacco tamper. No competitor is allowed to poke and probe the tobacco in his pipe, nor can he (or she) use a pipe cleaner once he has lit up. He mustn't move the tobacco in the bowl by blowing down the pipe or by juggling with a tamper - originally a tool used for mixing clay. It is not very clear what you *can* do with it. Competitors have five minutes to fill their pipe, and two minutes to light it with the two matches allowed them. And then it's 'Time's up; no more ignition; the competition is under way!'

'Will you please leave the table !'

Everyone has the same weight of tobacco, either three and a half or four grams, and presumably the same brand. They sit four to six at a table headed by a Table Steward who makes sure they all play the game. He tells anyone who can't 'make smoke' after 60 seconds from lighting up, to withdraw from the competition and leave the table.

Most of them can be expected to keep their pipes alight for 90 minutes, but the winner may well make non-stop smoke for two hours. Anything over 60 minutes is 'commendable'.

The winner of the National Pipe-Smoking Competition may be asked to represent Britain as a member of the St Bruno team in an international competition, which in one year took place in Japan.

Pipesmoker of the Year for the **joy** of it

Not that they have to demonstrate their smoking skills round a table under the eyes of a Steward, those who for 12 months can call themselves Pipesmoker of the Year are chosen by members of the tobacco trade, however, for their known pipemanship and the joy they get from it.

Now organised by the Pipesmokers Council, Pipesmoker of the Year awards have been made since 1964 - see list.

PIPEMEN OF THE YEAR

1964 Rupert Davies
1965 Sir Harold Wilson
1966 Andrew Cruickshank
1967 Warren Mitchell
1968 Peter Cushing
1969 Jack Hargreaves
1970 Eric Morecambe
1971 The Rt Hon The Lord Shinwell
1973 Frank Muir
1974 Fred Trueman
1975 Sir Campbell Adamson

PIPEMAN OF THE DECADE
1976 Sir Harold Wilson

1977 Brian Barnes
1978 Magnus Magnusson
1979 J B Priestley
1980 Edward Fox
1981 James Galway
1982 Dave Lee Travis
1983 Patrick Moore
1984 Henry Cooper
1985 Jimmy Greaves
1986 David Bryant
1987 Barry Norman
1988 Ian Botham
1989 Jeremy Brett
1990 Laurence Marks
1991 Sir John Harvey-Jones
1992 Tony Benn
1993 Rod Hull
1994 Sir Ranulph Fiennes

PIPEMAN OF THE CENTURY
Lord Shinwell

Flute-Pipe to smoke sideways

Britain was the first country to honour its leading pipe smokers. Awards are presented at a luncheon which the public can pay to attend, the proceeds going to charity. In recent years each award winner has received a pipe appropriate to his calling. James Galway got a miniature flute with gold keys which could be smoked sideways.

Pipemen of the Year: James Galway 1981

Pipe Pleasures Start Here

The Pipesmokers Council was formed in 1978. Its activities are funded by the principal pipe and tobacco manufacturers in the UK. Michael Butler is its secretary, and it is administered by an executive committee who are selected for their wide range of national and international experience, and for their specialist knowledge within the industry.

Its main object is to promote pipesmoking. In 1989 it published Britain's first guide to tobacconists, THE PIPESMOKERS WELCOME GUIDE, updated every year. In 1991 it ran a national cartoon competition on pipesmoking. Tobacconists were lent 50 of the best entries to exhibit in their shops for a week or two at a time. The Council distributed some 250,000 copies of its booklet PIPE PLEASURES START HERE.

But most smokers know the PSC as the body that organises the always widely publicised Pipesmoker of the Year project.

5

A LITTLE OF WHAT *You fancy*

A woman is only a woman

Conventional, down-to-earth mortals, like this clean-cut character of yester-year in his smart suit, would have had no truck with 'fancy' pipes, but got all the pleasure in the world from smoking a conventionally shaped, down-to-earth model. That's what he fancies.

But here he is smoking acigarette.

This is Rudyard Kipling (1865-1936), author of all those Jungle Books and Barrack Room Ballads, a smoker all his life, who compared the short pleasure to be derived from smoking a cigar unfavourably with the longer lasting pipe.

There's peace in a Laranga,
there's calm in a Henry Clay;
But the best cigar in an hour is
finished, and thrown away.
A woman is only a woman,
but a good cigar is a smoke.

A little of what you fancy does you good.

'It suits you!'

And here is the Smoaking Hussar again - his pipe suits him too, doesn't it ?

It all adds up to the same thing - delight - whether it's

'His pipe is his one extravagance.....'

across the sitting room for Carpet Slipper Alf in his arm chair

or across the desert for Carpet Bagger Ali on the other side of the hill.

These pipes won't suit ANYONE

EVER CONCEIVED BY MAN
(OR AT LEAST THE 10 WORST THIS WEEK!)

POPCORN-COB
KERNELS POP FROM HEAT OF THE BOWL!

BREAKS IN LIKE A DREAM – SMOKES SWEET AS A NUT!

SUPER CHURCH WARDEN

THE FARTHER THE SMOKE HAS TO TRAVEL, THE COOLER IT IS.

50 FEET OF TUBING CONNECT BOWL & STEM IN THIS MODEL

BREAKS IN LIKE A DREAM ETC.

WHEN FRIENDS EXAMINE THIS MEERSHAUM PIPE'S BOWL, THEY GET AN UNEXPECTED SURPRIZE!

WORLD'S FIRST EVEN-COLOURING MEERSHAUM

(FILL IN BLANKS)
BREAKS IN LIKE A ____, SMOKES SWEET AS A ____

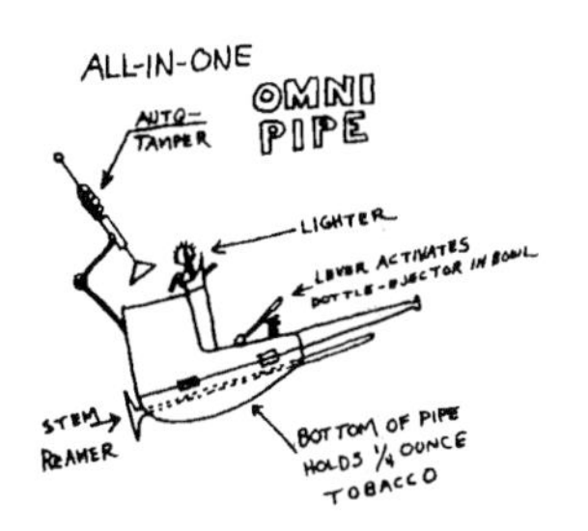

SMEETS SWOTE DREAMLIKE NUTS!

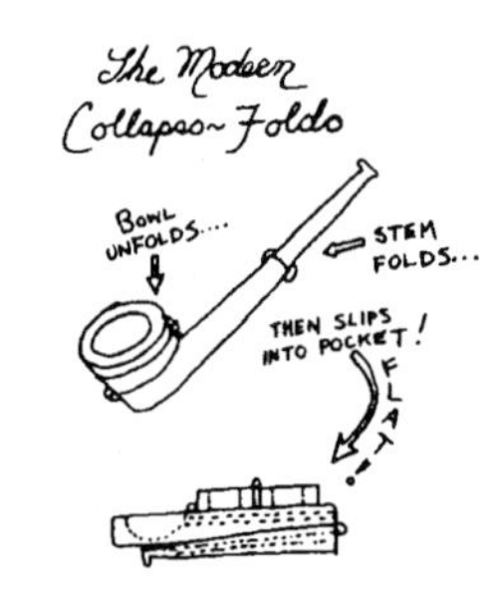

BREAKS IN – SMOKES AS PER USUAL

A DREAMLIKE NUT BREAKS IN SWEETLY SMOKING

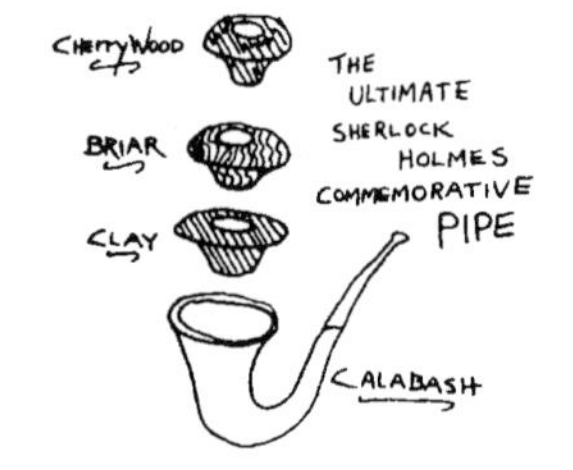

SHOULD SATISFY ALL SHERLOCKIANS

CALABASH WITH INTERCHANGEABLE BOWLS OF THE ONLY THREE TYPES VERIFIABLY SMOKED BY S.H.

WHILE SMOKING THE NUT DREAMED OF A BREAK-IN

DUOPIPE
"IT'S DOUBLY DUMB"

SNAP-A-STEM

WHEN YOU BITE THRU THE STEM, SIMPLY SNAP IT OFF TO REVEAL A NEW ONE!

SNAP-OFF STEMS

BET YOU CAN'T GUESS WHAT IT BREAKS IN LIKE, OR SMOKES SWEET AS!

B.I.L.A.D. – S.S.A.A.N. (FOR THE LAST TIME!)

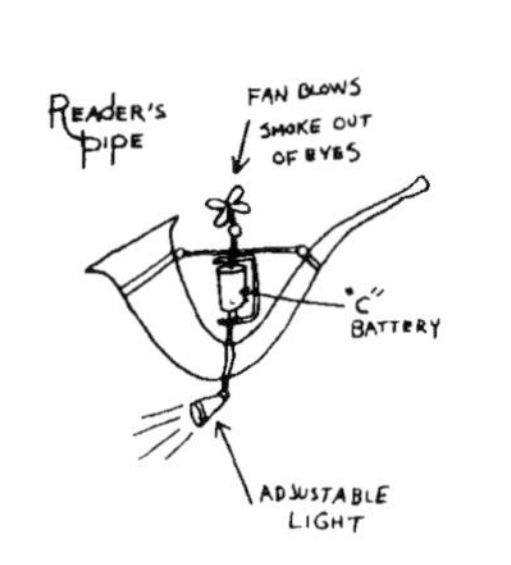

Break a Neck

As you will hear from John Phillips of Weingott in Fleet Street (established 1859), from whom you can still buy a clay pipe 1990s-version, in the Old Days the landlord of an alehouse kept a stock of crude, no-frills, clay London Straws, suited to the likes of his crude customers who would not feel comfortable with anything remotely frilly.

Clay pipes

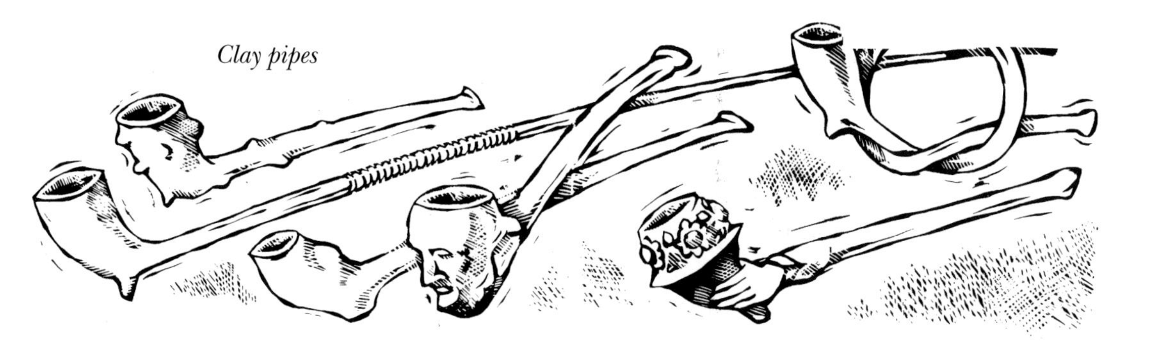

The frilly sort - not for porters

The pipes were 'on loan' to anyone who came in. All they had to do was to take a pipe from the stack, fill it and light up. When they had had their smoke and pint of porter - many of them were thirsty porters for whom the drink had first been brewed - the publican retrieved the pipe, broke off the bit that had been in the smoker's mouth and threw it away. He then put the pipe, that much shorter, back on the pile for the next man. Chain smoking.

'Go away, woman ! Can't you see I'm busy ?'

Satire on the self-indulgent clergy 1773.

No clergyman, who hoped he could ever again persuade his parishioners to pay their tithes, would ever allow himself to be seen in an alehouse. It was bad enough having to put up with an old gossip from the village poking her nose into his study - and what a nose ! - while he was enjoying a puff or two in private and a quaff or three of whatever liquor was in that elegant bottle.

Invariable pleasure

WITH A COUNTENANCE GREATLY MOLLIFIED BY THE SOFTENING INFLUENCE OF TOBACCO, REQUESTED HIM TO 'FIRE AWAY.'

Sam Weller was never one to be ashamed of enjoying life to the full, which meant, among other things, draining what that girl has brought him, a double glass of 'the invariable' (whatever that was made up of), and puffing away at his clay pipe in front of the fire with, as his creator Charles Dickens describes it, 'critical solemnity'.

That was all in the Old Days - the Good Old Days.

The modern look suits YOU

IF YOU WANT to put one over the Rangers fan next door who thinks he's impressing you with his hand-carved, straight-grain briar pipe – "nothing to do with the briar rose, you know" – and the Celtic fan on the other side who bores you with stories of the meerschaums his grandfather left him, from one of which the smoke issues from Napoleon's hat and the other from Jeremiah's beard; if you want to shame them for being behind the times, produce your Vestpocket – "made specially for me last week, you know" – which fits snugly into your waistcoat pocket. You deftly demonstrate how the mouthpiece can be turned back on the bowl. One-upmanship, eh?

Vestpocket

On your feet or on your bum?

A LOT DEPENDS on what sort of pipe suits standing up and what sitting down. For this lover boy, anxious to keep his feet on the ground while writing to his mistress, a long stem is highly suitable. For this artist, anxious to keep ash smudging his carefully painted reflections, nothing else will serve the purpose but a short stem.

When a sitter stands

'Bubbles' by Sir John Millais, Bt.. PRA

WHEN A SITTER INSISTED on standing – and, what is more, turning her back to him – it was obviously a comfort for a portrait painter like Sir John Millais to be able to add to the pleasure of making a good job out of an unpromising subject, that of smoking his pipe.

It will have been a sacrifice for Sir John to deny himself the pleasure of puffing smoke into the air when his sitter was a little boy who sat blowing soap bubbles into the air. Several years later the boy had become an admiral and switched to pipes.

GOES WITH THE JOB - GOOD ONE OR BAD ONE

SMOKING HAS FOR LONG been an accompaniment of whatever you happen to be doing at the time, whether painting a lady's backside, favouring a quayside with your company by lounging about it waiting to become the oldest inhabitant, like the fellow on the right, or going topside - 'Smokers upstairs, *if* you please!' - and answering silly questions from civvies such as I suppose you always smoke Navy Cut ?, like the weather-beaten sailor on his last day of leave below. Like Millais, making the best of a bad job.

New Curate (to village gossip). *'Don't you think it's about time your son learnt some trade?'* Village Gossip. '*Bless yer 'eart, no; e's all right, 'Is father 's done very well this many a year as oldest inhabitant, and 'e'll just step into the business when the time comes.'*

On church business

NOT ONLY CHURCHWARDENS but church vicars and curates, not to say bishops, smoked on the job. Dr Bull, the High Church Bishop of St David's, watched the passing through Parliament of the Security of the Church of England Bill of 1707, 'sitting in the lobby of the House of Lords, all the while smoking his pipe'. And not a murmur from their lordships sitting beside and around him.

And of course the same goes for the Friends of the Clergy, not the sort of people to take chances on their staying power, only that of horses.

A country curate, c. 1793

A sketch near Piccadilly

A PROPOSAL A LA MODE.
'Well, old scream, what about it?'

But it was a cigarette while on the serious business of popping the question

The toff engaged in the arduous task of trying to change the situation from merely 'walking out' to 'being engaged' also smoked on the job.

But for him of course it was a cigarette, and fixed firmly in a long, expensive and hopefully impressive cigarette holder.

And it seems to be working. Her eyes are certainly on it. Whether Old Scream knew what he meant by 'it' is another matter.

THE INSPIRATION FOR PROFESSOR MANHESEL'S SMOKOMETER ?

Enjoying the aroma of the chauffeur's cigar.

Smoking tobacco burnt at a distance ?

Was this man, whose name has not gone down in history, the inspiration for what Professor Manhesel, a German of great vision, called his 'Smokometer' ?

Perhaps the professor happened to be walking up the pavement beside the taxi when he noticed the cabby in front of the glass partition, with cigar smoke billowing from his mouth, and then, glancing at his bushy-haired fare in the back, saw to his amazement that he was snuffing up from the tube rather than talking down it? 'Aha!' said the professor, or its German equivalent, 'tubed tobacco smoke ?' If Friedrich Winzer (a German compatriot) got away with conveying coal gas, generated by burning coal in a gas-works, in pipes under the street from a central gasometer to houses for gaslighting and gas cooking, could he not do the same thing with tobacco gas/smoke ?

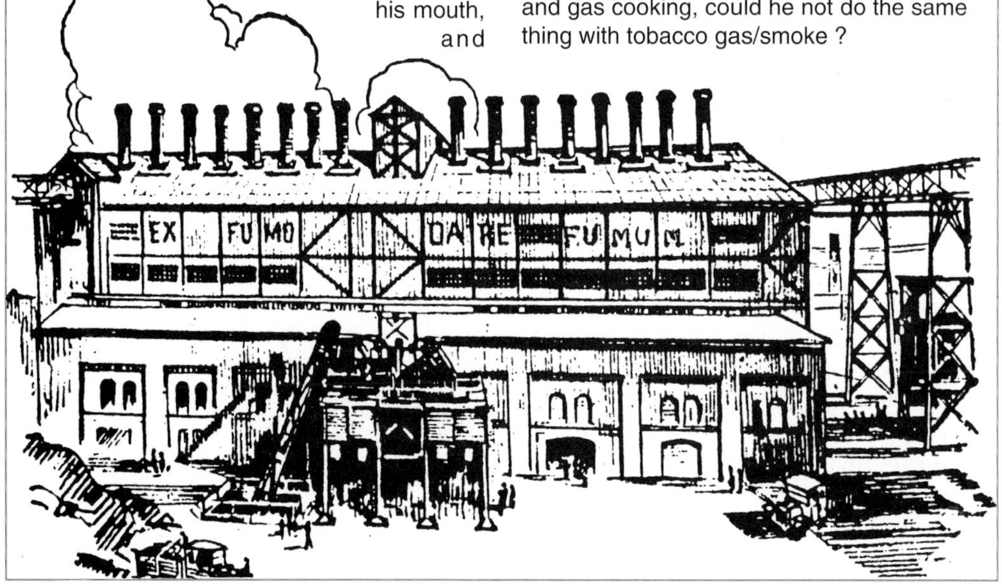

Manhesel's dream

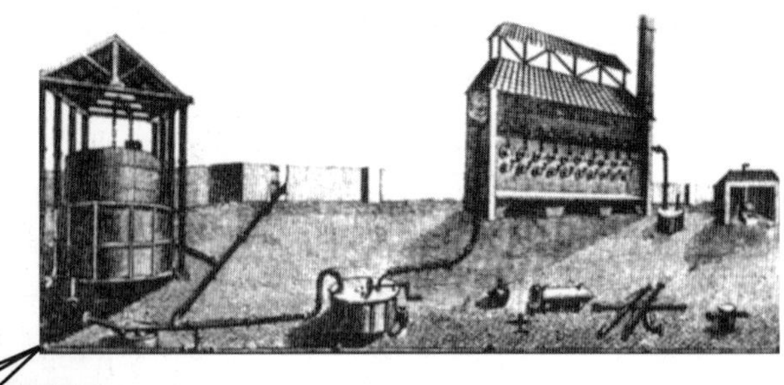

Manhesel proposed erecting a large works on tobacco plantations in America, and piping tobacco smoke by the cubic foot to houses in the neighbourhood. He planned to burn tobacco in large retorts, and pipe the smoke to a huge bell-shaped chamber, a 'Smokometer' where it would be cooled, purified and scented. From there the smoke would be conveyed in pipes below the streets to houses, each of which had its own small reservoir which would take and hold its own piped supply of tobacco smoke. From there pipes would take it to rooms terminating in long flexible tubes with amber mouthpieces. The smoker turned on a tap (like on a gas fire), put his mouth to the mouthpiece and drew instant, ready-made tobacco smoke.

Smoke-on-Tap

Smokometer fitters installing a Smoke-on-Tap system in West Bromwich ?

Regular maintenance of course was going to be essential if the stream of smoke could always be relied upon to reach the mouth from so distant a source.

Since those operating the Smokometer would be hard tempted to siphon off free smoke from a pipe in the works, it was realised that the place would have to be designated a Smoke-on-Tap-But-Not-For-You Area from Day One.

PIPE-CLEANER.

Smoking Suit

For the pipe smoker not to have to do all that pushing and pulling with his own cotton and wire pipe cleaner, which had a secondary role of satisfying his creative urges as a wire manikin artist; not to indulge personally in the filling, poking, probing, scraping and tampering processes, in the match striking and blowing out; in the lighting up and subsequent knocking on the ashtray; for the cigar smoker to be deprived of doing the crackle test behind the ear - none of this gave them reason for opting out of the dressing up which for so long had all been part of the ritual fun.

You didn't have to carry your dressing up as far as this Maya priest. Wearing some sort of special livery, however, that seemed suited to the rituals of smoking made withdrawal to the Smoking Room even more pleasurable. You changed your long tail coat for a short more comfortable Smoking Jacket. The French followed suit and called any kind of short dinner jacket Le Smoking. Some added a Smoking Cap; the jacket tended to become draped. Then with 'dressing for dinner' done less and less, the demand for Le Smoking fell away. It ceased to be fashionable; though Robert Gieve of Gieve & Hawkes will tell that he still has orders for them.

Maya priest smoking

Torch bearer

Smoking Dress is not to be confused with Fancy Dress.

How long do you think it took this stalwart employee of British-American Tobacco to make this egg-shaped costume, composed of BAT cigarette cartons, for a fancy dress party in Jaffa (in what was then Palestine) in 1924 ?

How long did she have to stand in it once she had managed to get it on ? All night, presumably. She can't have sat down on it. 'Some Cigarettes, Some Egg' reads the plaque on her bosom. Some stamina, more likely !

Seventy years ago people who worked for British cigarette firms in far corners of the world were willing to stand up for - well, if nothing else, for enjoying themselves the hard (and stiff) way.

The man's a bounder - but at least he's taken the band off

IF FEW FEEL LIKE wearing smoking jackets these days, they have no choice when it comes to conforming to smoking etiquette at a formal dinner, like not lighting up before the royal toast.

You will see, in this famous H M Bateman cartoon, that all the unlit cigars which still lie on the table have their paper bands round them.

Here lies another piece of etiquette, which at least that bounder, who has dropped a clanger by lighting up before the toast master had had his say, has followed: Never smoke a cigar with the band on. Some, however, will tell you that the band was put there to keep the leaves tight and compact; and that if you try and take it off when the cigar is cold you risk breaking it. Leave it on until the cigar warms up, and it shrinks and the band loosens to make it easier to remove.

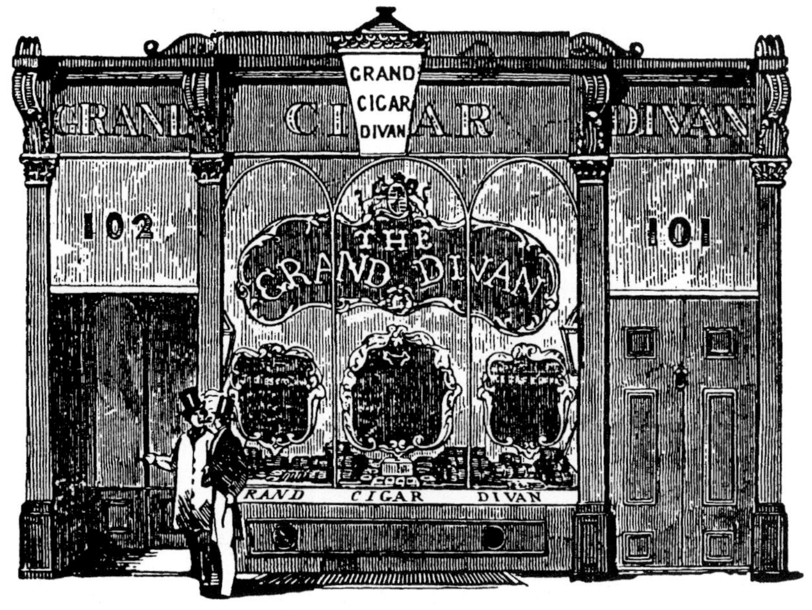

Simpson's
. Strand .
A Century
. . Ago . .

ORIENTAL STRAND

Upmarket cigar shop where upmarket gent, who made downmarket social gaffe at that upmarket banquet, bought his gaffe-making cigar, was probably from a 'Divan' like this one in the Strand.

Apart from meaning a draped couch or sofa built into the wall at the raised rear end of a room on which lay sultry seductresses with loose kaftans and even looser morals, Divan was also the word for a Smoking-Room furnished with couches on which smokers could lounge, and then for a Cigar Shop.

No standing on ceremony for this poor fellow. In a few minutes, when he's finished that last gasper, he won't be standing on anything.

In Singapore

they were less patient

'M-m-mm - I like the commercial!'

What chance a pipeful of peace?

While the man on the scaffold is firmly on course for making peace with his maker, the descendants of the original inhabitants of North America - which Christopher Columbus called Indians because he thought he had landed in India - were pursuing a less certain track in trying to make peace with the descendants of their 'discoverers'. Inviting them to draw smoke with them, through a shared Pipe of Peace, had its drawbacks. Once the pipe went out, would all the goodwill it had generated be snuffed out too? It was a brave ploy, but no sure fire hope of succeeding.

Today the goodwill symbolism of a Pipe of Peace has tended to be obscured by other considerations.

'It says: "The Surgeon General Warns That Smoking the Peace Pipe May Be Harmful to Your Health." '

IT DIDN'T REALLY HELP A BRITISH PRIME MINISTER EITHER, SEEING WHAT HE WAS SITTING ON.

ABERDEEN SMOKING THE PIPE OF PEACE

Smokers not suckers

Interior of a Smoking Tavern (Tabacie) in London in the Time of the Stuarts

'Do we want any lollipops? You must think us a lot of suckers. We're a smokers' club. Get out!'

6

EVERYBODY'S DOING IT, DOING IT, *Doing it*

The Man in the Street

When Stephen Potter, inventor of the science of getting one-up on the next man in sport, love, business or whatever, listed the various types of people one was likely to encounter in walking down life's highway, he saw the Typical Individual, the Representative Male, the Man in the Street (code name LUDLOW), dressed and behaving like Most People, as sitting there - you see him below - in a tweed jacket, baggy trousers, club tie, hands in pocket and - smoking a pipe.

Mr Average, just part of the landscape.

ONE-UPMANSHIP BUSINESSMANSHIP

Type Three, LUDLOW, is the tremendously ordinary chap, valuable because he is in close touch with tremendously ordinary people and can, himself, talk tremendously ordinarily. We can't do without Ludlow, because he is the man in the street.

DIAGRAM OF MAN IN THE STREET

Type Four, MAIDENHAIR, we draw especial attention to because he represents a totally new type, of high value, as we believe, and something we are perhaps rather specially proud of, because he has been developed entirely through Life-manship-sponsored organizations. He is the man not in the street. Sometimes he has taken a First or possibly read a biography of Verdi.

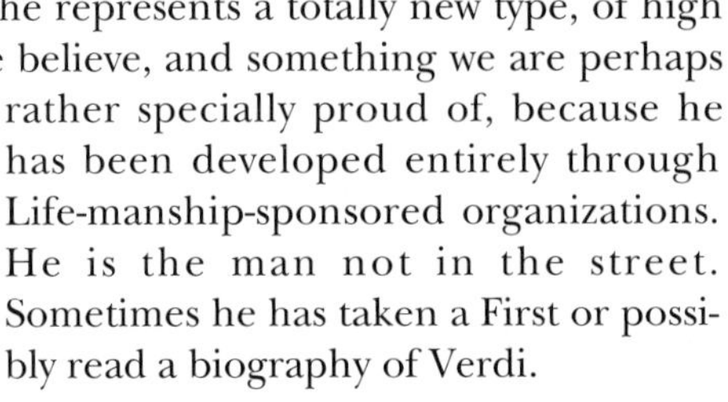

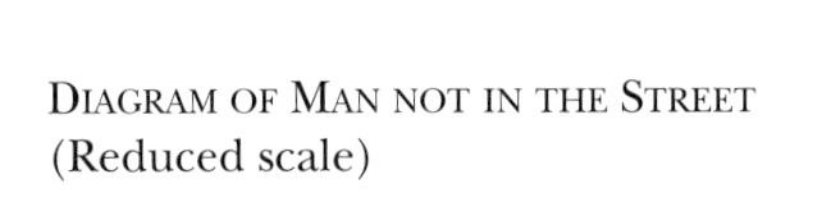

DIAGRAM OF MAN NOT IN THE STREET
(Reduced scale)

The Man in the Stadium

Out of one hoop into another - that's life!

And then aaah! - that's the Hamlet Moment which, for the Man in the Stadium - and now on his way out - will make up for all the unfortunate entanglements he's got himself into in the course of the most embarrassing fifteen minutes of his life.

The Man in the Boxing Ring

Henry Cooper, Pipesmoker of the Year 1984

The Man in the Cricket Field

The Man on the Screen

Groucho Marx smoking a *pipe*?

Yes.

Before appearing with his equally zany brothers in films, Groucho performed on stage in musical comedies on Broadway, New York, such as this one, *I'll Say She Is,* in 1924.

The more familiar cigar by which he is known by cinema fans all over the world was just as much a stage prop as his moustache - one never saw him light it.

Or perhaps *you* did?

Baggy trousers,
cane, bowler hat and - cigarette

FOR CHARLIE CHAPLIN smoking was never part of his Little Tramp character in the way that that cigar was part and parcel of Groucho Marx.

But here, in the cover of this piano music sheet, the Little Tramp has the familiar cane in his right hand and the unfamiliar cigarette in his left.

Like Groucho, Charlie Chaplin was a stage comic before making films. In 1911 he appeared in Chicago with Fred Karno's London Company in a sketch called A Night in a London Club based on another Karno sketch The Smoking Concert. Chaplin was the drunk intruder who makes havoc of all the acts.

Smoking Concerts could be riotous fun

Smoking Concerts could be rowdy and bawdy forms of amateur entertainment, even (in Edwardian days) in the would-be sedate setting of an Oxford college. Undergraduates vied with each other to see who could be more daringly risqué in the 'patter' between songs.

After a Smoking Concert at Brasenose, patter which infuriated the Principal ran:

You know my sister Annie. She's a bad girl. At dinner the other day Mother said to her 'Annie, if you do that again I shall smack you.' And Annie answered, 'You can't Ma, I'm sitting on it.'

After that, the learner-comedian was told he would never be allowed to appear at a college Smoking Concert again.

Bottoms were out - outrageous

Bottoms were unmentionable, but no harm in obesity. At next year's Smoking Concert, Paul Rubens, a University College undergraduate, sang a song with the lines:

She was fat, she was fat,
She was awful, awful fat;
She weighed at least some twenty stone in nothing but her hat.

Whereupon the Principal turned to his neighbour and said, 'What I like about Paul Rubens is that he is so amusing without being at all vulgar.'

Joy for world-class operatic tenors

AMATEUR SMOKING concerts were not for the likes of these three. Enrico Caruso (1872-1921) (*right*) was the most famous opera singer of his day, seen here with two other stars of Italian Opera. All of them enjoyed a smoke, as you can see from what they are holding in their hands when posing for this photograph.

The Man on Stage

'HOW COME NO MATCHES, HOLMES?'

'Elementary, my dear Watson. My wind-protected cigarette lighter-cum-ashtray does the job better when, as I find myself doing now and then, pursuing hounds with luminous eyes across windswept moors.'

How come Sherlock Holmes is smoking a *cigarette* instead of the pipe which is his trademark? is what *you* are probably asking. No mystery. The camera never lies. The evidence is in this rare photograph of American actor/dramatist William Gillette playing the great detective at the Lyceum Theatre in London in his own stage play *Sherlock Holmes* which he wrote in 1899. On a British tour of the play in 1903 14-year-old Charles Chaplin played the part of Billy the page-boy. 'Pull down the blinds, Doctor. I don't care to be shot from the street this evening' is the caption to the photo.

Disguised as a clergyman? Something diabolical is afoot.

Smoking off-stage

A year after Master Chaplin's first appearance on the stage was born John Gielgud (right), destined to become a stage and film actor of equal renown, still active and acting in 1994, seen here smoking, out of costume at home, one of his favourite Turkish cigarettes - something he has done all his life. 'His superb tenor voice remains unimpaired and instantly recognisable,' observed *The Observer* on the occasion of his 90th birthday. Sir Alec Guinness said it was 'like a silver trumpet muffled in silk'.

Sir John Gielgud's contemporary Sir Ralph Richardson was not only an actor of great distinction but an intrepid motor-cyclist. In the latter role he could have done with one of those wind-protected lighters which William Gillette is holding in that photograph, which would have enabled him to stop his pipe going out without stopping.

MEN ON THE FRONT BENCH

'What did I tell you about smoking in front of the Minister, darling?'

One cannot but admire men-in-the-street, who volunteer to take a part in governing themselves and us, by becoming elected to Parliament and then being chosen to sit on the Government front bench as ministers in an Administration to which we lend them, for the duration of that Parliament, the power to issue orders restricting this, prohibiting that, and warning about the other thing. What a strain it must be to strike a balance between personal delights, and what they and their advisers conceive to be the Public Good ! to avoid accusations of 'overkill', 'over the top'.

Ruskin Spear's 1974 portrait of Labour prime minister Harold Wilson leaves no doubt in the eye of the beholder of the nature of *his* delight.

TONY BENN, PIPESMOKER OF THE YEAR 1992, BY TROG

EMANUEL SHINWELL
1884-1986

NOTHING PARTICULARLY 'LEFT WING' ABOUT PIPE-SMOKING

Stanley Baldwin, seen here (right) in a 1936 caricature by Tony Wysand, with his son Oliver, was three times Conservative prime minister between 1923 and 1937, and died in 1947 aged 80. Neither he nor Harold Wilson, Labour prime minister between 1964 and 1970, seen behind that cloud of tobacco smoke, ever had occasion to air their views on Smoking and the Public Good in an official capacity. In their time it was not 'an issue'.

'From having been a cigar smoker - rarely a pipe - in his early manhood,' wrote Baldwin's other son Windham in his biography of his father, 'with the war came the wish to deny himself some of the luxuries he had enjoyed hitherto. He began to smoke more the less expensive pipe; and soon no other kind than a half-crown cherry wood did he care to use for the rest of his life.'

Smoking out Peculiarities and Absurdities

THE SMOKING ROOM has for long had the reputation of being the part of the Palace of Westminster most frequented by the wits of the day expounding their views on every issue, from the threat of women becoming mayors to the health dangers of lighting, cooking and heating by gas.

None more consistently than Henry Labouchere, MP for Northampton and founder of the scandal-exposing magazine *Truth.* 'Labby', as he was known, could never stay in his seat in the chamber for more than a quarter of an hour, 'dashing out for a whiff of smoke, rushing back for a whiff of politics, out again, in again, and so on.' He was seen and heard at his best in the smoking-room of the House of Commons where, seated in an American rocking chair smoking interminable cigars, he would tell stories and discourse on political conspiracies, and hit off in biting phrases the peculiarities and absurdities of all leaders, irrespective of party.

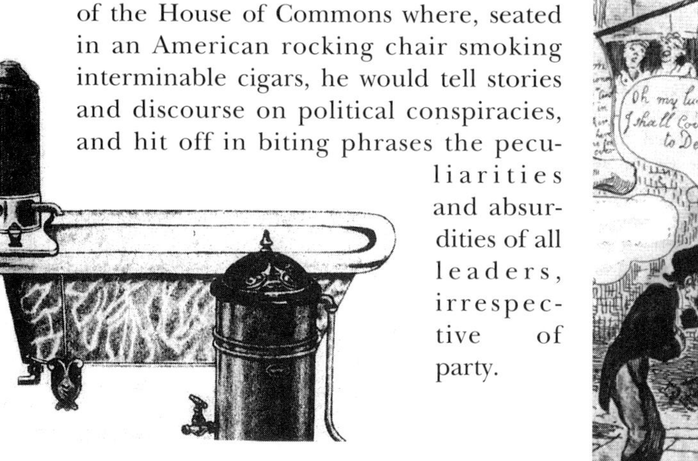

The ill effects of gas soon paled in the light off its benefits; and anyone expressing horror at the prospect of Lady Mayors was thought peculiar and absurd.

Pipe dream... Lord Mason, the former Labour cabinet minister, surrounded by fellow pipe-smoking peers outside Parliament exercising their freedom to smoke, on No Smoking Day yesterday. (*The Guardian*, 10 March 1994)

'Sherbert lemon, anyone?'

Puffing Peers

TODAY, 15 peers and 19 MPs of both political parties, with Lord (Roy) Mason, the former Labour cabinet minister, as Convenor, meet informally three or four times a year as The Lords and Commons Pipesmokers Club (Trevor King, Secretary). They visit exhibitions of pipe-smoking memorabilia such as the Sherlock Holmes Museum. They attend in force the annual presentation of Pipesmoker of the Year Awards, and gather every year to protest against the Government's No Smoking Day. In 1993 they went to Calais to note the differences between French and British pipe tobacco.

As Nelson said to Lady Hamilton...

Smoking politicians and top brass have for long been a traditional feature of British parliamentary life.

Look at this satirical cartoon of 1800 of the Lord Mayor of London entertaining William Pitt the prime minister, Admiral Lord Nelson and others, whose words issue from their mouths in clouds of smoke.

On the extreme right Emma Hamilton complains to Nelson of her elderly husband's failings as a lover - 'Pho! the old man's pipe is allways out, but yours burns with full vigour.' 'Yes, yes,' answers the virile seadog, 'I'll give you such a smoke, I'll press a whole broadside into you.'

Beneath the Lord Mayor with his huge looped pipe on the left, sits a dog on its hind legs smoking a pipe beside tins of tobacco.

Small Dogs, Big Dogs and Big Cats love it

Cartoonists love smoking dogs.

'"Household pet," yes..."ordinary," no.'

And this leopard obviously has no wish for his furry headed GP to change his smoking habits, only his spots.

'Oh yes, we can change your spots. It's quite an operation, but we can do it'

Grrrisly

Grisly types like this, sitting on their backsides outside their cave, who one moment will be hugging a bottle of stout and the next moment, if you are foolish enough to anger them, will be hugging *you*, give themselves an air of affability by smoking a pipe.

Slimy

More cultured toads wishing to forget their former pond life, and in an attempt to erase their slimy image, re-assume tails, and gesture in a grand way with a smoking cigar which, however, as you see here, so often smoulders away in their hand, fanned by the wind in the willows from which they can never entirely escape.

Another shaggy dog story

'Smoking and wallowing in self-pity, please.'

'Second door on the right, sir. But one moment. What about that noisy dog you've got with you ? I have a responsibility to protect my customers from passive barking.'

BARKING UP THE WRONG TREE

They left Monty at the desk, which only added to their self-pity, and on their way down the passage to the room marked S & S-P, behind two others heading for the same destination, they overheard one turn to the other and say, 'But I thought you were turning over a new leaf ?' To which his companion replied, 'Oh no, I'm sticking to the tobacco I've been smoking since 1954.' And the humourless income tax inspector, who was coming up behind them, was far from amused to find himself a passive laugher.

If you are as confused as we are about this, turn over the page.

7

COULDN'T YOU ~~CAN'T~~ HELP *Laughing*

Naughty Boy

'We give you Henry for your enjoyment' J Wix & Sons told their customers. Also for their enjoyment was the fine Virginia tobacco in the 'Kensitas' cigarettes to which Henry was linked.

The pranks that hairless, egg-headed Henry got up to - 50 in all - were aimed at endearing smokers to this particular brand of cigarette around 60 years ago - between July 1935 and March 1937. You couldn't help laughing at his ingenious plan to earn a dishonest halfpenny by painting Meesols spots on the faces of his chums, to get them off school. All in the never-fail comic tradition of Just William.

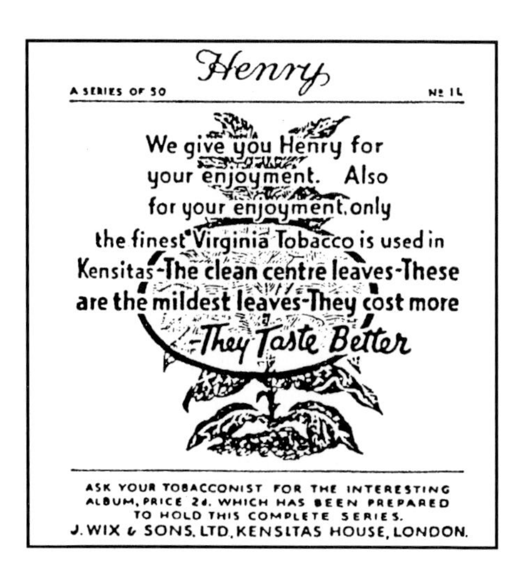
Henry
A SERIES OF 50
Nº 1L
We give you Henry for
your enjoyment. Also
for your enjoyment, only
the finest Virginia Tobacco is used in
Kensitas - The clean centre leaves - These
are the mildest leaves - They cost more
- They Taste Better
ASK YOUR TOBACCONIST FOR THE INTERESTING
ALBUM, PRICE 2d. WHICH HAS BEEN PREPARED
TO HOLD THIS COMPLETE SERIES.
J. WIX & SONS, LTD, KENSITAS HOUSE, LONDON.

TO THE
DOCKS
CEMENT

Henry
Henry
Henry
Henry

THE GENTRY

Top hatted Mr Gold and Mr Flake, 'Men with Wills of their own', started their promotional lives in 1927, and carried on punning and joking for the next two years. Sample joke:

'Why are Wills Gold Flake like a pretty girl, Mr Flake ?'

'I know Mr Gold, Because they never get left on the shelf. That's why they're always fresh.'

The first of a long series of advertisements featuring Mr. Gold and Mr. Flake which ran from 1927 to 1929

Julius Wix took the same line, but below stairs, with Jenkyn the Butler, to promote 'Kensitas' cigarettes. Jenkyn was created by Wix's advertising agents Ralph Winter Thomas & Co in 1920. At the British Empire Exhibition at Wembley in 1924, Wix had a Kensitas stand, on the front of which stood a real life Jenkyn in the person of an actor looking and dressed like the butler in the drawing.

THE HALL MARK OF FINE QUALITY

Ten years later, Kensitas introduced Empire Flag Cards printed on silk, followed the next year by silk Flower Cards.

These Capstan Shanties, of which there were 21, appeared in the Illustrated Weekly *publications in 1937 and 1938*

Riddles

Mr Gold and Mr Flake's riddles have a long ancestry, as this advertisement, at least a hundred years old, testifies.

Whether the answer to the question, 'Why is a window like a star ?' lies in the picture, is itself a riddle. There must be *some* significance in the bespectacled farmer (?) tying a cord from his pig's leg to his umbrella, on to which rain is pouring down while he reads a newsheet called *Court Journal* and hastens away from a tombstone with an indecipherable inscription. But whether it contains the answer is another matter. Come to think of it - that is, *you* come to think of it - Why *is* a window like a star ? Your guess is as good, or bad, as ours.

And then again

Why *is* London Bridge like the House of Lords ?

A prize for the best answer ?

You must be joking.

Tag lines

HAMLET MOMENT

Happiness is . . .

Light an Abdulla.

TOBACCO.

A MONTHLY JOURNAL FOR

Tobacco Traders and Tobacco Smokers.

No. 1.] {VOLUME I. / REGISTERED FOR TRANSMISSION ABROAD.} JANUARY 15TH, 1881. [THREEPENCE.

TABLE OF CONTENTS.

IMPORTANT SALE AT LIVERPOOL.

By Public Auction, on WEDNESDAY, 26th inst.,
At 11 o'clock, at the
BROKERS' SALEROOMS, IMPERIAL CHAMBERS, 62, DALE ST., LIVERPOOL.
TOBACCO:
570 Hds. and Tierces American Leaf and Skips,
(With a view to meet the requirements of Manufacturers and Exporters)
450 Bales and Cases, China, Turkey, German, Dutch, &c.,
And Sundry Lots of Cavendish Cigarettes, &c.

CATALOGUES OF
EDWARD SAMUELSON & Co., Brokers & Factors.

J. HIGGINS,
PIPE STEM MANUFACTURER,
Importer of Foreign Pipes,
AND EVERY ARTICLE FOR SMOKERS.

PIPES MOUNTED AND TUBES REPAIRED.
Agent for the Real Scotch and Irish Clays.

124, Aldersgate Street,
LONDON.

IMPORTANT TO MANUFACTURERS OF IRISH ROLL.

PURE OLIVE OIL,
Guaranteed Genuine and Sweet,
In Tins, Barrels, or Casks,
AT THE LOWEST POSSIBLE PRICES.
JOHN R. RHODES & CO.,
IMPORTERS AND REFINERS,
Offices: Barton Arcade, Manchester, and Park Oil Works, Cheetham.

ESTABLISHED 1865.

SAMUEL M^c LARDY,
PIPE MANUFACTURER,
AND
Importer of Tobacconists' Fancy Goods,
16, MILLER STREET,
MANCHESTER.

ALL THE NEWEST GOODS AS THEY COME OUT.

MANUFACTURER OF THE
Torrified Clay Pipes for West Coast & Cape Trade (Africa).
ANY DESIGN MADE TO ORDER.

ILLUSTRATED & DESCRIPTIVE CATALOGUES ON APPLICATION.

DUTCH CIGARS.
WELL KNOWN AS THE
BEST CONTINENTAL PRODUCE.
First-rate quality exported by
LADNER & CHARDON,
AMSTERDAM.
General Agent—
RICHARD SHAW,
ALBERT BUILDINGS, PREESON'S ROW
LIVERPOOL.

W. & C. PAGE,
TOBACCO, SNUFF & CIGAR MANUFACTURERS,
Grange Tobacco Works,
GRANGE ROAD, BERMONDSEY, LONDON, S.E.

W. & C. P. beg to draw attention to the undermentioned Special Goods:
W. & C. PAGE'S 'PRIZE MEDAL'
GOLD CUT HONEYDEW,
Guaranteed as a perfectly pure Tobacco, cut from the finest selected leaf, beautifully rich in aroma.
W. & C. PAGE'S CELEBRATED
SMOKING MIXTURE,
A carefully selected combination of the choicest Tobaccos, cool and fragrant.

SPECIAL AND FANCY TOBACCOS CUT TO ORDER
Full Price List on Application.

Unjokey advertisements in the first issue of *Tobacco* magazine (15 January 1881), still publishing in 1994 under editorship of Jacques Cole. 'Torrified' means moisture removed.

Cuddly advertisement

AN EARLY ADVERTISEMENT
Father says 'Must be Wills's'

Two-handed Advertisement

for hats (left hand) and tobacco (right hand)

For stiffening not promoting

Whether finding a cigarette card inside the pack ever substantially boosted cigarette sales between the 1890s and the 1940s, they never failed in their prime purpose, which was to stiffen the pack. To the tobacco trade, these cards, at first plain white with no printing or picture on them, were always 'stiffeners'.

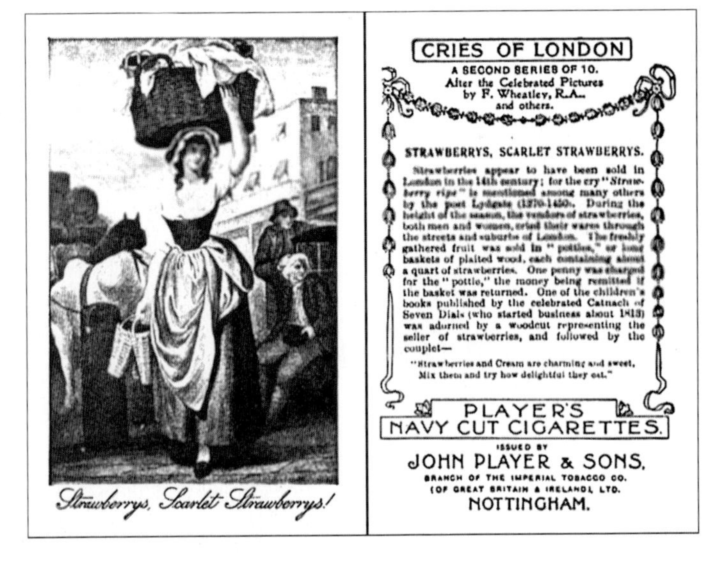

A break came in 1887 when a stiffener was put into a Wills pack with a printed advertising message in red and black, and the following year they put a picture on it as well, of a pack of Gold Flake. Their first non-advertising pictorial card, featuring ships and soldiers, with a one-line caption and nothing on the back, appeared in 1895. The next year's series of cricketers had a picture on the front and a CV of the players on the back. In 1897, when Queen Victoria celebrated 60 years on the throne - her Diamond Jubilee - Wills issued a series of Kings and Queens of England, and Her Majesty bought a set printed on satin.

Double Meaning Sayings

Whoever had the job of thinking up subjects for new series of cigarette cards, after the obvious ones like Flags and Flowers, Footballers and Floosies had been exhausted, earned full marks in 1898 with his 52 Double Meaning Sayings.

At that time the boneshaker, which made the derring-do automobilists sneer at cyclists as Cads on Castors who were always getting under their wheels, had just given way to the Improved Safety Bicycle. Hence one Double Meaning, illustrated in this series, was A Safety Match - two cyclists racing.

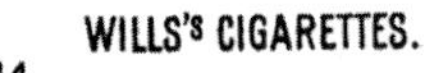

THIS SURFACE IS ADHESIVE ASK YOUR TOBACCONIST FOR THE ATTRACTIVE ALBUM (PRICE ONE PENNY) SPECIALLY PREPARED TO HOLD THE COMPLETE SERIES

SAFETY FIRST

A SERIES OF 50

7

OVERTAKE ONLY WITH SAFETY

Never overtake unless you can see sufficiently far ahead to do so with safety. It is dangerous to overtake on bends, at cross roads, when approaching pedestrian crossing[illegible] streets and on h[illegible] bridges—the drive[illegible] car in our pictu[illegible] grave risks. N[illegible] on any road wh[illegible] line marked do[illegible] overtaking n[illegible] part of your v[illegible] the line. The[illegible] justification [illegible] hicle (except [illegible] Before overt[illegible] self that it i[illegible] never " cut[illegible] œuvre.

W.D.&[illegible]

ISSUED BY T[illegible] (OF GREAT [illegible]

Samples of Others:

Brothers in arms - a nurse holding two babies

A model wife - her husband painting her portrait

Wills for Quality

4TH SERIES OF 50.

31

DO YOU KNOW the origin of Margarine?

Margarine is the legal name for any substitute for butter, *which resembles butter and is not milk-blended butter*. The name (derived from the Greek *margaron*, pearl) was given by the French chemist Chevreul, but the article was first manufactured on a considerable scale during the Franco-Prussian War by another French chemist, Mège-Mouriès, whose portrait appears on the other side. Since then this food product has been greatly improved, and the Margarine manufacturer of to-day aims to produce artificially (from refined vegetable oils), a substance which upon analysis has the same formula as butter. The difference between the two lies chiefly in the *kind* of fat, not in the *quantity*.

W.D.& H.O.WILLS

ISSUED BY THE IMPERIAL TOBACCO CO (OF GREAT BRITAIN & IRELAND) LTD

All cards from the collection of Edward Wharton-Tigar

Can't Have Beethoven, He's An Enemy Alien

When Britain declared war against the Kaiser's Germany in August 1914, with France as her ally, Wills promptly withdrew their 'Waterloo' set of cigarette cards. 'Since it would have been tactless to remind the French of this previous defeat, the issue was cancelled' states Roger Till in his book *Wills of Bristol.*

They also took out the German and Austrians in their 'Musical Celebrities' set, and replaced them with 'Allied' musicians.

When Edward VIII abdicated in 1936 they felt they had to cancel the 50-card series they had prepared depicting the stirring events of the King's life as Prince of Wales.

One in the series of *Punch* cartoons issued by Wills during the First World War of 1914-1918.

Just before the outbreak of this war, Wills had prepared a series of 'Musical Celebrities' which included eight German musicians which were withdrawn in August 1914. One of these was the composer Meyerbeer who had died in 1864. All eight cards were replaced by ones of non-German musicians. The same policy was adopted with regard to German music being played at the Promenade Concerts at Queen's Hall.

Don't just stick'em in, *flick'em out*

NON-SMOKING BOYS made sure their fathers never threw away the cigarette card/stiffener with the carton. If there was going to be any throwing, they would do it but not into dustbins.

Most built up collections and stuck them into albums which the tobacco companies made available through tobacconists. Boys would swap cards, of which they had more than one, for others they needed to make up a series, much as they did with postage stamps.

Another way of adding to the collection was by playing a game against a wall. They tossed a penny to see who would go first and then, each in turn, flicked a card at the cards against the wall. The first boy to hit a card took all three of them plus all those that had missed and lay on the pavement.

BE READY FOR AIR ATTACK

When it looked as if a Second World War was going to break out and the German airforce would start bombing Britain's cities, the Government told people how to prepare for them by taking Air Raid Precautions - ARP. Wills helped the authorities get their message across by issuing a series of 40 ARP cigarette cards.

Cartophilists'

FOR A TIME cigarette card collectors never managed to call themselves anything other than Cigarette Card Collectors. But then, not to be outdone by stamp collectors who had thought up the impressive word 'Philately' to describe what they were doing, leading enthusiasts formed what they called The Cartophilic Society of Great Britain.

HE HAS
The Largest Cigarette Card Collection
IN THE WORLD

A boy who started collecting cigarette cards at the age of four in 1917 - his first was of corn-crake in a British Birds series - in 1994 is indisputably the owner of The Largest Cigarette Collection in the World. Edward Wharton-Tigar has more than a million of them - from Boer War Heroes, Chinese Nudes, Humming Birds of Hawaii and Nineteenth Century Serving Girls to the History of Hungary, the Preservation of Poultry and Tips for Air Raid Precautions.

He has bought out many of the world's other collections, including that of Charles Matthews of Staffordshire, Britain's largest pre-war collector.

After dangerous adventures as a Special Operations Executive agent in World War 2, in the 1950s he became managing director of the international mining group, Selection Trust. He is now retired - well, sort of.

The world's No. 1 Cartophilist, in 1948 he became Research Editor of The Cartophilic Society and set about cataloguing every cigarette card that had ever been printed. Phew !

He has bequeathed his collection to the British Museum.

Edward Wharton-Tigar

Moving picture CIGARETTE CARDS

You couldn't have collected the moving picture cigarette cards which took over from the pack stiffeners in the shape of television 'commercials' in the nineteen sixties. But Gallaher themselves made a collection - or rather a selection - of the best of their Hamlet series on a video cassette, introduced by comedian Willie Rushton.

Their last tv commercial was screened in October 1991 when Britain had to conform with the European Economic Community's ban on television advertising of any kind of tobacco product.

For 27 years some 80 short films set out to tell us at home or in the pub that happiness was a cigar called Hamlet.

We saw seemingly well-adjusted individuals confronted by situations that would unnerve the best of us, if not send us round the bend and off our rockers probably, but not Gallaher Man who, when all else spells unhappiness finds it in . . . you know what. Like Ronnie Cobbett up there coxing the sinking eight in the Varsity Boat Race on the Thames.

A PUFF IN TIME SAVES... WELL, ALMOST ANYTHING

They were a valiant lot, those tv heroes of the Hamlet saga - a frustrated King Canute whom the tide would not obey; a Bird Man whose wings let him down only too painfully; a Father whose glowing pride in paternity turns to pale horror as the expected one turns to unexpected four; a sad Voyeur who runs out of coins just as he gets the beach girl in the sights of his telescope; an Egyptologist who eases open the mummy's sarcophagus in the darkened tomb and finds himself facing a hand offering him the product . . . .

. . . . a non-starter jockey; a washed-out Pavement Artist; a thwarted Kubic Cube player; a sneezing matchstick Cathedral Builder; a Party-Goer who thought it was Fancy Dress; a bad Bunker Player; a Toupee Wearer who failed to apply sufficient fixative . . .

Talk of cool detach ment!

And there was the ghostly spectre of this unruffled Tudor Gent, with his head tucked beneath his arm, coolly smoking The Cigar in a gesture of carefree detachment from the worries of the world he left so long ago - reminiscent of the 100-year-old decapitation feat in the New York dime museum of the 1890s.

Which all goes to show there is nothing new under the sun and that it is an illusion to think otherwise.

Talking of illusions, have a look at the next page.

No matter he's short of magic flux

The moving pictures all tied in with the Hamlet Moment stills.

'Stuck up sort of chap that ! Thinks he's Lord Muck just because he's smoking a cigar. Good mind to leave him up there to teach him a lesson. However, a Hamlet has never let anyone down, so I suppose it's up to me. If only I wasn't losing my magic touch. (Thinks) If only I had a Hamlet to help me recover it.'

Do you think that's what he's thinking ? Well, something like that. A bit more down to earth maybe ?

The Cigar is not the only pebble on the beach happiness-wise

Jacky Fleming insists that

And no tucking into packets of junk food either!

Who knows what damage the person next to you on the Bakerloo will suffer from Passive Eating?

London Underground are doing their best to limit it with this notice:

PLEASE NO MUNCHING

HE'S NOT BEING PENALISED FOR EITHER MUNCHING OR SMOKING

There is also a steel cage . . . to protect them from the fury of ordinary travellers.

The man in the steel cage next to the guard's van on the train from Woking (1930s version, as you can see from the guard's Southern Railway uniform) is a share-shuffler who has been put there by the guard to protect him from the fury of fellow travellers, such as the one with clenched fists, on whom he has gone to work during the journey. Now, with the aid of a cigar, he is wondering what went wrong, and considering what line of attack he should take to make his next day's operation from Tonbridge less likely to result in another incarceration.

Locked In And Silent *until . . .*

Talking of incarceration, J B Morton, in another of his 1930s Beachcomber columns, tells how the offer of a **CIGARETTE** broke down the social barrier between two businessmen locked in a giant safe, who had not been introduced and could not therefore converse.

For several hours they crouched in the safe without saying a word to each other. One tried to break the ice by suggesting they were at the same school. He was wrong.

There was silence for another hour, and then the Harrow man offered the Etonian a cigarette.

'That's awfully decent of you,' said the Etonian.

And then they began to thaw.

After two hours they had invented a game of cricket with a handkerchief rolled into a ball and a fountain pen for a bat. When the safe was opened they were arguing amicably about a leg-bye.

8

FRINGE Benefits

On the fringe, that is, of the central object of the exercise, which is to give pleasure to the smoker - benefits to people and activities not directly concerned with smoking.

But before we turn to that, let's look at the aspect of that central pleasure which sets it apart from so many other pleasures, namely that you can indulge in it *without using your hands*. Once you've got rid of all the lighting business, your hands are free to get on with giving yourself enjoyment by another means *simultaneously*.

Look at this chap on his push-bike. Admittedly he's overdoing it by not using his free hands to guide the bike, but then he's just showing off. His swanky display in no way detracts from the point that anyone can enjoy a cigarette and ride a bike - and, at a pinch, beneficially keep his hands warm by putting them in his pockets.

AND THIS LITTLE MAN
talking to the Baked Tater Merchant can
truthfully say, without (much) boasting,
that he can enjoy smoking his pipe *and*,
not only keep his hands warm, but the
top of his head too.

For musicians it's one pleasure at a time - except for this one.

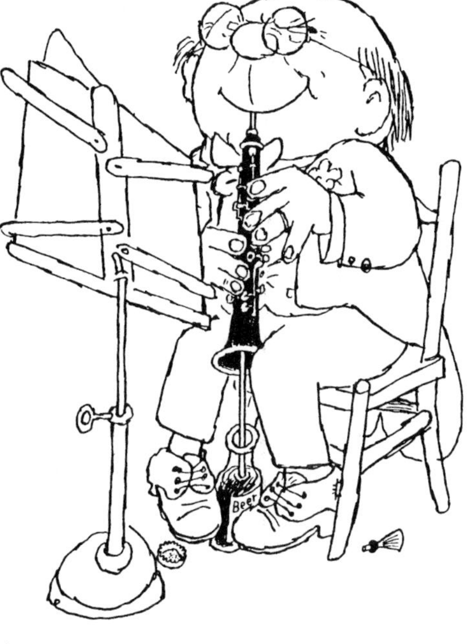

The musician who gets pleasure from playing his instrument is stuck with it. Both hands are fully occupied. They can't do anything else - unless they belong to one who has devised a way of simultaneous beer-siphoning and oboe-playing. But he is not typical.

On the other hand, a smoker can smoke *and* play golf; can smoke *and* ride bareback on a circus horse. He's showing off too, but then he's in show business.

The Whitebait Cycle

An ingenious contraption necessitated by the exorbitant charges for hire of boats at the seaside this season

W Heath Robinson

See what we mean?

A Thing of the Past

AND OF COURSE you never needed to be without the pleasure of smoking by having to apply your hands to keeping upright on being swept off your feet (in the days when smoking was allowed on the Underground) when a packed rush-hour train began behaving erratically.

Doesn't Stop You Joining in the Bunfight

AND YOU NEVER needed to deprive yourself of the pleasure of smoking in order to take an active part in any general mayhem that might suddenly break out in the back parlour.

'You and your churchwarden. I've told you I don't like smoking in the bathroom!'

SMOKING *under water,* **in water** and ***by water*** **(SALT)** *and* by water **(FRESH)**

A GOOD COMPANION - IN HIS BATH

Popular author, dramatist and smoker Jack Priestley (right) used both hands to write his best-selling novel of the nineteen thirties *The Good Companions* and all his many other books and plays; and admits to getting particular pleasure from smoking away from his desk.

Long after the others have caught the 8.20 and opened the morning mail, I am lying in my hot bath smoking a pipe. I am not even soaping and scrubbing but simply lying there, like a pink porpoise, puffing away. . . . I am lost in steam, the fumes of Latakia and the vaguest dreams.
(*Delight,* 1925)

BY WATER (SALT)

'Arry. 'Come over the other side, Alf, and see a big sailing-ship pass.'
Alf (faintly). 'You can 'ave it. Call me - when you see a tree pass.'

BY WATER (FRESH)

HAMLET MOMENT

LITTLE DROPS *of* WATER, LITTLE GRAINS *of* SAND, MAKE THE MIGHTY OCEAN *and* THE PLEASANT LAND

- and make havoc of American humorist Robert Benchley's efforts to enjoy a quiet smoke on the beach.

At the end of four minutes standing on the beach with his hands above his head, there was always sand in his pockets, on the back of his neck, inside his trouser waistline and in his pipe. 'It is marvellous' he wrote in his essay *Sand Trouble*. 'Smoking is one of life's pleasures which is easiest marred by this little trick of sand. After a swim in the ocean or lake there is nothing more refreshing than the tang of tobacco smoke, yet the risks incident to lighting a pipe are so great it is hardly worth while. A pipe is particularly susceptible. You can wait until you have had your swim and then have a man come down from the bathhouse with a fresh pipe in a chamois bag which he himself can insert in your mouth (naturally, not still in the chamois bag), and which he can light for you with matches also brought freshly to the beach, handled only with silk gloves.'

- but the sand was still the winner, filling the stem so that his teeth were a-grit.

Drinking *and* pouring smoke

Smoking has given conjurors a whole host of ideas. One of the simplest is the Liquid Smoke Trick. He takes a mouthful of cigar smoke, puffs it into a glass and then 'pours' it out of one glass into another like a liquid. He shakes the glass and 'drinks' it as if it was a Smoke Cocktail. Maybe he blows a big smoke ring, and a smaller one right through it. Aaaah !

These are little more than 'parlour tricks', but sophisticated apparatus lies behind making a chosen playing card, returned by the chooser to the pack, find its way into a cigarette case. And of course only a professional can do a proper job with a smoking ventriloquist's dummy.

It's easier to light up if you haven't got a head.

Plucked *lighted* cigarettes from the air

MANUAL DEXTERITY - the very opposite of the Look No Hands! act of that chap on the bike - is the secret of conjurors who specialise in plucking lighted cigarettes out of the air one after another.

Frakson sent showers of sparks from the ends of the cigarettes he produced.

AN EARLY PERFORMER of this kind was a Spaniard called Gili Jose Florences who, after presenting his act throughout Europe and South America, appeared in New York in 1914 billed as 'Something New in Magic'. It was a claim he justified with his pioneering routine with lighted cigarettes.

A GREAT ADMIRER of Florences was another Spaniard Jose Jiminez Seville who, as 'Frakson', introduced the continuous production of lighted cigarettes into vaudeville - music hall, as we called it in Britain. His tour of Europe, when he was billed as 'The Man With 100 Cigarettes' included a long engagement at the London Palladium. When he went to the USA he thought it would be more sensational to call himself

'The Man with 1000 Cigarettes.'

Sorry - can't tell you how they do it

John Calvert starred in several films, as well as his magic show.

The Frenchman Pierre Cartier, who performed similar tricks in France under that name, and in England, including Variety at the London Palladium, as Keith Clark (*above* and see poster), wrote an *Encyclopaedia of Cigarette Magic* and another book called *Celebrated Cigarettes*, both published in the USA in the 1940s and for eyes of professional magicians only, explaining the techniques. Chris Woodward of The London Palladium Theatre Collection had the encyclopaedia till May 1994, but then sold it to a man in America. So no revelations - as if the Magic Circle would have let us anyway ! Cartier/Clark died in the 1970s, but American illusionist John Calvert, a cigarette manipulator extraordinary, is still active in 1994, so is another, Englishman David Berglas. Robert Harbin, who changed his cigar into a pipe, died in 1978.

The "Ace" of Conjurors
CARDINI
HOUSTON SISTERS
WRIGHT & MARION
The Cheeky Chappie
MAX MILLER

A Lighted Meerschaum Appeared *from* Nowhere

THE MOST CELEBRATED and original cigarette magician of them all was also an Englishman, Richard Pitchford, born in Mumbles in 1899. He learnt card tricks in the trenches in the Great War, and when it ended he became a professional conjuror and ventriloquist. He specialised in card tricks, which he did wearing gloves, and took the stage name of Cardini.

HE DEVELOPED AN ACT in which he walked on as a tipsy, monocled swell in white tie, tails and top hat, in whose gloved hands appeared one pack of cards after another. He then steadied his hand, and with some effort fitted a cigarette into a holder in his teeth. The cigarette kept disappearing and re-appearing. He finally lit it with a lighted match that fell into his hand. Lighted cigarettes began plaguing him one after the other, and a final lighted cigar. As he strolled off, a large lighted meerschaum appeared from nowhere. He seized it and made his exit smoking it.

PRESIDENTS ROOSEVELT AND TRUMAN were among his fans. During a ten-month engagement with the Crazy Gang at the London Palladium, he did his act before George V at the 1933 Royal Command Variety Performance. He was well named The Suave Deceiver.

Cardini devised and presented an act and a style that has never been surpassed.

You too can be a *Cardini* - by collecting *Carreras* cigarette cards

If, as a boy or girl, you had seen Cardini performing at the London Palladium or Glasgow Empire, and come back with a burning ambition to follow in his footsteps, you could have made a start on the road to stardom by collecting the Carreras cigarette card series of 50 'Amusing Tricks and How To Do Them'.

UNSPILLABLE MATCH BOX

AMUSING TRICKS & HOW TO DO THEM

A SERIES OF 50

No. 37

UNSPILLABLE MATCH BOX.

Have two matchboxes, about half full, and give one to your friend, saying, "Do exactly as I do!" Rattle your box. Partly open it, at each end, revealing the matches inside. Turn your box face down on the table, carefully drawing off the outer cover, leaving the inner case bottom upwards. Lift your inner case a few inches. Your companion, following your example, will drop his matches.

METHOD.—Prepare your own box by wedging a broken match across the middle, as shown.

CARRERAS LTD.

(ESTD 1788)

How about no 37 the Unspillable Match Box trick ? You'll have Uncle Fred completely mystified - you hope. And that over-fed, over-dressed Mr Oliphant from next door cannot but be impressed by your Sugar Torch trick (no 11) - or can he ? He won't be if the spot of cigarette ash you have put on the sugar lump, as the instructions on the back tell you, fails to ignite.

THE SUGAR TORCH

AMUSING TRICKS & HOW TO DO THEM

A SERIES OF 50

No. 11.

THE SUGAR TORCH.

Show your audience an ordinary lump of sugar and invite them to set fire to it with a match. They will be unable to do so. Now take back the piece of sugar and apply a match, whereon the sugar will burn with a light blue flame. (As burning drops may fall, a plate should be handy).

METHOD. — If you surreptitiously press a small spot of cigarette ash on the piece of sugar, you will have no difficulty in making it burn.

CARRERAS LTD.

(ESTD. 1788)

ARCADIA WORKS, LONDON, ENGLAND

KEEP THIS AMUSING SERIES OF PICTURE CARDS IN THE CARRERAS "SLIP-IN" ALBUM OBTAINABLE FROM ALL TOBACCONISTS. (PRICE ONE PENNY)

Then you'll have to persevere with the *Bewitched Walking Stick* (no 16) and the *Weeping Pencil* (no 25). Your mastery of all this mirth-making, uncanny magic will be the start of a career that will take you to an engagement, if not at the Palladium, at least for next year's Christmas concert in the church hall.

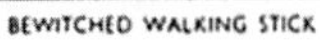

A SERIES OF 50

No. 16.

BEWITCHED WALKING-STICK.

Prepare by fixing two pins to the knees of the trousers and tying a long black thread to the two pin heads. Standing at some distance from your audience, show an ordinary walking-stick. Now, sitting down and opening the knees so that the thread becomes taut, place the stick against it. The spectator, to whom the black thread will be invisible, merely sees a walking-stick standing magically without support.

CARRERAS LTD.
(ESTD. 1788)
ARCADIA WORKS, LONDON ENGLAND.

KEEP THIS AMUSING SERIES OF PICTURE CARDS IN THE CARRERAS "SLIP-IN" ALBUM OBTAINABLE FROM ALL TOBACCONISTS. (PRICE ONE PENNY)

THE WEEPING PENCIL

A SERIES OF 50

No. 25

THE WEEPING PENCIL.

Borrow a long pencil. Place it behind your ear. Tell your audience that this pencil has always wanted to be a fountain pen, and relieves its disappointment by shedding tears! Your audience may scoff at this absurd story, but you can discount their scoffing by showing that the pencil actually weeps.

METHOD. — Have concealed behind your ear a small piece of wet sponge. Take this in the hand surreptitiously and press against the pencil, unseen by your audience.

CARRERAS LTD.
(ESTD. 1788)
ARCADIA WORKS LONDON, ENGLAND

KEEP THIS AMUSING SERIES OF PICTURE CARDS IN THE CARRERAS "SLIP-IN" ALBUM OBTAINABLE FROM ALL TOBACCONISTS (PRICE ONE PENNY)

Smoke Gets In Your Eyes -

But not from your cigarette but your heart which is on fire

Smoking has brought money and fame to songwriters, for so many of whom it has been, as an activity, an inspiration. The BBC Record Library has 50 titles with the word Smoking in them, and another 25 with Smokin'.

Contrary to what you may have assumed, the smoke in Jerome Kern and Otto Harbach's hummable number *Smoke Gets In Your Eyes*, which Irene Dunn sang in the film version of the Broadway musical *Roberta* in 1935, was not tobacco smoke. People in love, she pointed out, are blind, because when their heart is on fire the smoke from it gets in their eyes. Lord knows what that smells like.

But of course, like a lot of others, he'd got it wrong. Otto wasn't talking about THAT kind of smoke.

Songs that *have* referred to tobacco smoke include *Smoke Rings* which the Mills Brothers recorded; *Two Cigarettes in the Dark; While A Cigarette Was Burning, The End Of Me Old Cigar*, and a favourite of Maurice Chevalier's, *Cigarette*, which however was the name of the girl he was singing to,wasn't it ?

Telling a man's character from the way he smokes a cigar

Smoking has aided what Americans call 'shrinks' in telling a man's character. When Punch heard an American scientist claim this, they speculated that this probably meant that a man who snatched a cigar from someone's mouth, and smoked it himself, could be assumed to be of a grasping disposition; that a man who smoked a cigar right through without removing it from his mouth, a deep thinker. 'The man who accepts a cigar from a friend, lights it, sniffs and drops it behind his chair has no character worth mentioning.'

HAMLET MOMENT

'SHRINK REPORT' on above:

'I would say, from the reaction of this armed-to-the-teeth warrior to what must have been a disturbing experience, during a quiet afternoon's row in The Lake without his Lady, with that fake magician Merlin shouting at him from the bank and that frog jeering at him from the bul-rushes - namely not only not letting his cigar slip from his well-armed teeth but to have the presence of mind to blow three well-formed smoke rings - I would say that that shows a man of determined character of the kind kings are made of.'

Spy Detector

Smoking has played its part in the fight against organised crime, in counter-espionage and bringing to book power-crazed maniacs who seek to rule the world like Dr Nikola whose exploits Guy Boothby described in his thriller of that name.

Dr Nikola was run to earth in a Shanghai opium den posing as a pig-tailed Chinaman, his very thorough disguise exposed by the intrepid agent, who had been tracking him down since page 1, by pressing a lighted cigarette into the top of the sitting Dr Nikola's head. As he thought, the 'chinaman' felt nothing, since the burn had been not on his skin but on the leather base of his wig. The tactic proved what he already suspected

· **Gotcha!**

And how often in real crime detection, have police confirmed the identity of a suspect who has been careless enough to leave beside the body the stub of a cigarette on the floor, or ash in an ashtray, of a rare brand that he is known to favour, or leave the smell of it at the scene of the crime - or, if it is a she, leaving her known brand of lipstick stain on the stub.

Gotcha!

In a Mickey Spillane novel a hoodlum was stopped by 'flicking a Lucky in his eye'.

Gotcha!

Benefits for picnickers, silversmiths, ashtray, match and lighter makers, cork growers (once) and the English language

Smoking has been a benefit to the picknicking classes by keeping the midges away from them, and saving them from the irritation or worse of midge bites.

Smoking has given lucrative employment to silversmiths who received orders for inscribed cigarette cases and boxes of silver for presenting to retiring directors and staff; and to the makers of decorative lighters, petrol Zippo and butane gas.

Smoking has given ditto to ashtray makers, matchmakers (non-matrimonial) and (for a time but no longer) cork tree growers whose product, hitherto used for the cork tips of cigarettes, have now been replaced by simulated cork of plastic on which has been printed a 'cork' design from which smokers, it is hoped, will feel they are getting the Real Thing (which by 1994 few of them ever knew).

Smoking has given lustre to the English language by fathering commands like 'Put that in your pipe and smoke it!', a much more colourful phrase than Digest that if you can, which is what it means.

His tobacco pipe transformed Britain's fresh water supply system

Smoking's contribution to improving the Quality of Life is well illustrated by the role which Thomas Savery's tobacco pipe played in the development of Britain's fresh water supply system. Tom Savery was the captain of a gang of Cornish tin miners, whose operations in the 1680s was hindered by the water that collected in the deeper mines, which none of the available pumps could remove.

Putting his tobacco pipe in a pot of cold water to cool it, Tom noticed how the hot bowl of his pipe, rarifying the air in the stem, made the cold water in the jar 'spring through the tube of his pipe in a wonderful surprising manner.'

In 1698 he took out a patent for his 'new invention of raising water by the impellent force of fire.' This technique, of raising water from mines, was applied to bringing it to the surface from underground waterholes and rivers for the supply of fresh water to towns, before the application of steam by Newcomen and Watts.

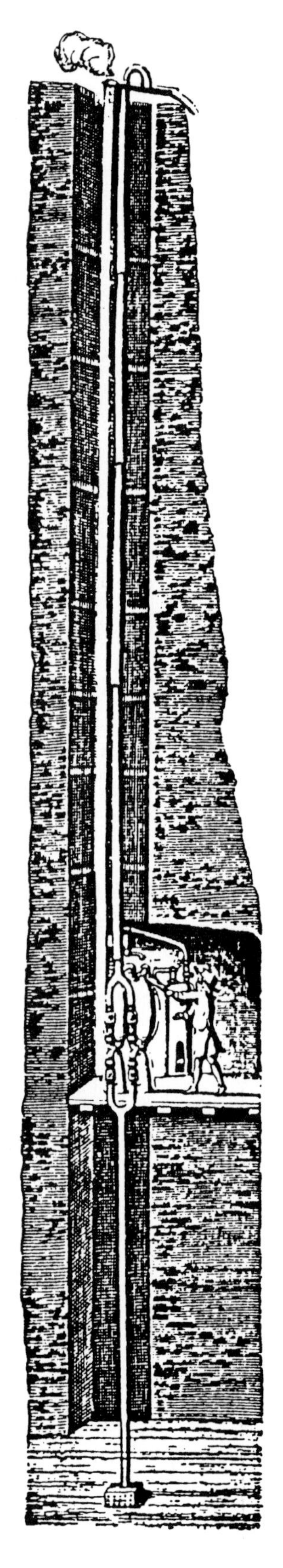

Tom Savery's water-raising invention in action

Smoking stimulates the nation's inventive powers

Motorist's ingenious wangle to light a pipe when the last match blew out

What pleasurable activity other than pipe-smoking could have roused this centre-of-the-road commercial traveller (to use an out-moded term) to apply his meagre mental powers to solving a problem from which most of his kind would have sheered away as being beyond them? Who knows, now that he has cracked this one, he will not feel confident to apply inventive powers, of which he had not been aware before the unforgettable Last Match incident outside Banbury, to other equally weighty problems, for the solution of which the nation will for ever be grateful ?

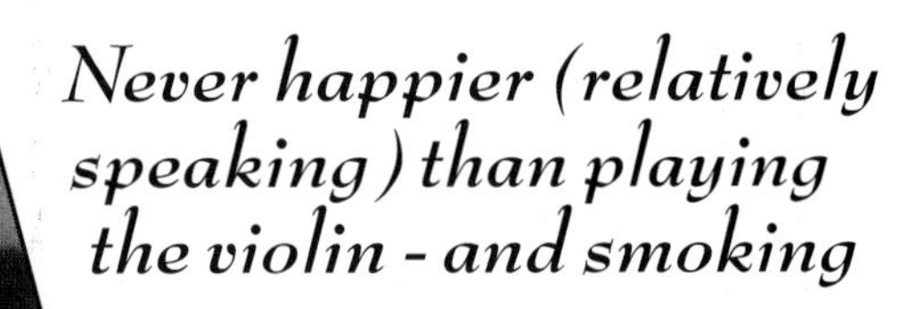

'My father's sole amusement was his pipe' declared a character in one of the sea novels of Frederick Marryatt, best known for his *Midshipman Easy*.

'And as there is a certain undefinable link between smoking and philosophy, my father by dint of smoking had become a perfect philosopher.'

A real life thinker who spent most of his life thinking out what real life was all about, was Albert Einstein (*above*) who did not become a philosopher by dint of smoking but, when not working on theories that changed man's view of the world we live in, took the greatest pleasure from playing the violin - and smoking.

Philosophy may not be up your street, but it was up this chap's, who lives up to everyone's idea of what a philosopher should look like, complete with pipe from which he got so much pleasure - Bertrand Russell.

HE'S NOT A *philosopher,*
BUT HE'S ACTING *philosophically*

HAMLET MOMENT

HE'S DETERMINED NOT TO *cave in.*

BUT THESE TWO JUST CAN'T *work it out*

WIZARD

Mumbo jumbo

And this character is obviously trying to work *something* out, and, when he has, to tell us the good tidings, presumably related to the tobacco he is flogging. Maybe, seeing he's wearing that apron, he is conveying a secret message to fellow freemasons, on the lines that the pleasure to be had out of smoking Carrington's needs as little demonstrating nowadays as any theorem of geometry as well proven as the one old man Pythagoras worked out all that time ago in ancient Greece about squares and triangles which he holds in his hand. Anyway, never mind about that. It's a decorative trade card, isn't it, whatever it means ?

What is Susanna's secret?

When it comes to being secretive Susanna beats the Carringtons man roll bowl and pitch.

But what *was* Susanna's secret? Who was Susanna?

She was an Italian countess living in Piedmont in the eighteen forties. She was the subject of the one-act opera, dubbed by contemporaries 'a musical trifle', *Il Segreto di Susanna*, which brought fame to its composer the Italian-German Ermanno Wolf-Ferrari (1876-1948) when it was first performed in Munich in 1909.

When Susanna's husband Count Gil smells tobacco smoke in the drawing room, he accuses his wife of entertaining a lover. She insists he has got the wrong end of the stick. Reluctantly she reveals the secret she has been harbouring for so long – that *she* smokes cigarettes. It cannot be! Yes, yes, it is the truth. Ahimé! No lover? Just an unladylike habit? Reconciliation, embrace, joy, happy smiles, curtain.

LIFE IS FOR LIVING

'I've never really learnt how to live, and I've discovered too late that life is for living.'

THE BBC'S FIRST DIRECTOR-GENERAL, AUSTERE SCOT SIR JOHN REITH.

'Though the human personality seeks perfection, its salvation lies in the effort not in the actual achievement. Perfection itself would mean death. Man cannot live for long on distilled water alone; he needs organic food, which would be useless to him were it not, by its nature, subject to decomposition and decay . . . Life is not Utopia. But it is life, and that is better than Utopia.'

LEWIS MUMFORD, *FAITH FOR LIVING* (1941)

'I run, I work out, I don't smoke, I only drink in moderation. If I weren't so smug about it, I'd be damn near perfect.'

© 1989 *USA TODAY*. Distributed by L. A. Times Syndicate.

John Witt

Words of Thanks

A lot of people have helped to put this book together, and we would like, in particular, to thank Miss Val Price, Miss Alice Morgan, Mr Ian Shepherd, Miss Liz Walker, Mr Vivian S Rose, Mr Phillip Shervington, Mr Clive Turner, Mr David Drummond, Mr David Berglas, Mr Ian Birks, Mr Christopher Woodward, Mr Edward Wharton-Tigar, Mlle Annette Beyer, Mr John Phillips, Miss Julie Robertshaw, Mr Anthony Burton, Miss Alice Laird, Mr Simon North, Mr Michael Butler, Mr Peter Wiseman, Mr John Fisher, Miss Jane Shrimpton, Mr Jacques Cole, Mr Bill Heard, Mr George Gay, Mr David Bacon, Mr Peter Middleton, Mr Trevor King, Mr Clive Humm, Mr I D McOmish, Mr Christopher J Mercer, Mr John Williams, Mr Richard Burney, Mr Ben Welsh, Mr R J W Gieve, Mr Brian Matthew, Mr John Whitehorn, Mr Andrew Kirk, the Cultural Attaché of the Embassy of the Federal Republic of Germany, and the staffs of Tunbridge Wells Public Library, the Guildhall Library, the British Library, Bristol Record Office, the Hulton Deutsch Collection and the Mary Evans Picture Library.

A lot of reading has also been involved, in such books as David Robinson *Chaplin, His Life & Art* (Collins, 1985); John Ellis, *World War II: the Sharp End* (Windrow, 1990); Annette Beyer, *Faszinierende Welt der Automaten* (Callwey Verlag München, 1983); Roger Till, *Wills of Bristol*; Barry Pain, 'Cigarette-Card History', *B.A.T. Bulletin*, 1928/9; A J Cruse, *Cigarette Card Cavalcade* (Vawser & Wiles, 1948); Andro Linklater, 'Tales of Sabotage and Cigarette Cards', *Telegraph Magazine* 12 February 1994; John Mulholland, *Book of Magic* (Cassell, 1963); *Benson & Hedges One Hundred Years 1873-1973*; Richard Gordon, *The Alarming History of Medicine* (Sinclair-Stevenson, 1993); Andrew Boyle, *Only The Wind Will Listen* (Hutchinson, 1972); Compton Mackenzie, *Sublime Tobacco* (Chatto & Windus, 1957); P G Wodehouse, *Over Seventy, An Autobiography With Digressions* (Herbert Jenkins, 1957); Michael Bateman (ed), *The Man Who Drew The Twentieth Century* (Macdonald, 1969); Milbourne Christopher, *The Illustrated History of Magic* (Robert Hale, 1975); W Heath Robinson, *Let's Laugh* (Hutchinson, 1940), *Heath Robinson Devices* (Gerald Duckworth, 1977); A Tindal Hart, *The Curate's Lot; Ripping Yarns, True Tales of Old Australia* (The Five Mile Press, 1992); B W E Alford, *W D & H O Wills & the Development of the UK Tobacco Industry 1786-1965* (Methuen, 1973); Count Corti, *A History of Smoking*, trans. Paul England (George G Harrap, 1931); Peter H Mack, *The Golden Weed* (Newman Neame, 1965); Tage Voss, *Smoking and Common Sense*, Paul Redfern editor (Peter Owen, 1992); J B Priestley, *Delight* (Heinemann, 1949); John Smyth, *In This Sign Conquer* (A R Mowbray, 1968); *B.A.T. Bulletin; Wills's Works Magazine/Wills's Magazine; Navy Cuttings* (John Player & Sons).

"I DON'T KNOW WHAT GIVES YOU THE MOST PLEASURE ... SMOKING IT OR JUST HOLDING IT!"
BENIAN.

Picture Credits

Page iii: Bill Caldwell/*Daily Star*. Page vi: A. Singleton/*The Spectator*. Page ix: Gary Larson. Page 1: 1992 calendar of the Greek League for the Protection of the Personal Rights of Citizens. Page 2: *top*, Tony Reeve; *centre and bottom*, H M Bateman/Heather Jeeves. Page 3: *top*, Joe Minacki/*The Wall Street Journal*, 29 November 1988; *centre*, Dale Carpenter/*The Wall Street Journal*; *bottom*, Sax, *Happiness is ... The Best of the Hamlet Moments* (Bloomsbury) © Gallaher. Page 4: *top*, © Mell Lazarus by permission of Mell Lazarus and Creators Syndicate; *bottom*, Rodney James. Page 5: from Count Corti, *A History of Smoking* (Harrap, 1931). Page 6: *top*, Clarke Hutton, *Byng Ballads* (Bodley Head, 1935); *bottom*, Greek calendar. Page 7: Jo Brown/*The Wall Street Journal*. Page 8: *left*, *Transvaal News*; *right*, Guildhall Library, Corporation of London. Page 9: block of 3 Wills cards *top, and bottom left*, Edward Wharton-Tigar; rest BAT Co Ltd. Page 10: *top*, Bert Thomas, *Punch*, 8 October 1919; *bottom*, H M Bateman. Page 11: *top left*, from *The Book of Benson & Hedges*: *right*, Pipe Smokers Council; *bottom*, Hulton-Deutsch. Page 12: Tom Dunn, *The Pipe Smoker's Ephemeris*. Page 13: *top*, Hulton-Deutsch; *centre*, *New York Post*, 28 October 1991; *bottom*, Pipe Smokers Council. Page 14: *top*, *Punch*; *bottom*, Hulton-Deutsch. Page 15: Gallaher, *Live in Peace*. Page 16: H M Bateman. Page 17: *top*, Pipe Smokers Council; *bottom*, Fred Jeffries, Pipe Smokers Council; Page 18: Tom Dunn. Page 19: Bill Lee, reprinted by permission Tribune Media Services. Page 20: *centre*, Rex F May, Baloo Enterprises; *bottom*, Tony Reeve. Page 21: Brant Parker and Johnny Hart. Page 22: *top*, Bill Lee, reprinted by permission of Tribune Media Services; *bottom*, Michael Atchison, *The Advertiser*, Adelaide. Page 24: *top*, Chuck Asay, reprinted by permission of the *Colorado Springs Gazette*; *centre*, Margulies © 1993, *The Record*, New Jersey; *bottom*, Jim Russell, *Sun-Herald*. Page 25: *top*, David Austin/*New Scientist*; *bottom*, Tony Reeve. Page 26: *top*, Richard Johnson, *New York Post*; *bottom*, Tony Reeve. Page 27: *top*, Jonse; *bottom*, *Chicago Sun-Times*. Page 28: National Portrait Gallery. Page 29: *Punch*. Page 30: from Gallaher, *Live in Peace*. Page 31: J H Dowd, *Punch*, 1917. Page 32: *top*, Bruce Bairnsfather, from *The Bystander's Fragments of France* (Imperial War Museum archive); *bottom*, 1917 postcard. Page 33: *B.A.T. Bulletin*, 1916. Page 35: Bruce Bairnsfather. Pagc 36: *B.A.T. Bulletin*, 1915. Page 37: *top*, Fougasse, *Punch*, 1917. Page 38: *B.A.T. Bulletin*, 1917. Page 40: Neil Bennett/*The*

SPECTATOR. Page 41: *top*, Steve Gatherem/*THE WALL STREET JOURNAL*; *centre*, Dedini/*THE NEW YORKER*. Page 42: *top*, Tony Reeve; *bottom left*, Demot Richard (Richie), Heusden, in *KARTOENBOEK "IK ROOK, EN DAN"* (Kritak, Leuven, Belgium/Les Belles Lettres, Paris); *bottom right*, Thomas Kerr, *NEW YORK TIMES*/*TOM DUNN'S EPHEMERIS*. Page 43: *top*, Steve Best (Bestie), donating fee to Roy Castle Lung Cancer Research Appeal; *bottom*, Matt/*TELEGRAPH MAGAZINE*. Page 44: *top*, Summers/*INTERNATIONAL HERALD TRIBUNE*; *bottom*, United Media New York/Knight Features London. Page 45: *top*, Nick/*THE WALL STREET JOURNAL*; *bottom*, Harpur/*SUNDAY TELEGRAPH*. Page 46: *top*, Greek calendar; *bottom*, Andrew Chalmers, *THE GOLDEN WEED*, 1965. Page 47: *top*, *PUNCH*, October 1988; *bottom*, Tony Reeve. Page 48: *top*, Ray Billingsley/*WASHINGTON POST*; *centre left*, Chon Day, reprinted with permission from *MODERN MATURITY*, © 1993, American Association of Retired Persons; *centre right*, Johnson, *NEWSDAY* (USA), 1 February 1990; *bottom*, Knight/*HERALD* (Melbourne), 8 February 1991. Page 49: *left*, Willie Rushton/*DAILY TELEGRAPH*, 29 March 1993; *right*, Mathys Dré, Kuringen/*KARTOENBOEK* – dream balloon, Pipe Smokers Council. Page 50: *bottom left*, catalogue of Decamps and Lambert from Annette Beyer, *FASZINIERENDE WELT DER AUTOMATEN* (Callwey Verlag München, 1983); *bottom right*, private collection of Annette Beyer, Zurich. Page 51: *top*, Decamps catalogue (Annette Beyer); *bottom*, Karl Ewald Fritzsch & Manfred Bachmann, *AN ILLUSTRATED HISTORY OF TOYS* (Abbey Library London) in the Bethnal Green Museum of Childhood. Page 52: from *RIPLEY'S NEW BELIEVE IT OR NOT* (Stanley Paul). Page 53: *top*, BAT; *bottom*, *PUNCH*, 1908. Page 54: from W T Moncrieff, *SONGBOOK*, 1834 (*PRINT AND THE PEOPLE 1819-1851*, Louis James, editor, Allen Lane, 1976) Page 55: from *THE BOOK OF BENSON & HEDGES*. Page 56: *top*, Guildhall Library, Corporation of London; *bottom*, Sir David Low, *YEARS OF WRATH, A CARTOON HISTORY 1932-1945* (Gollancz 1949)/Solo Syndication. Page 57: Harry Furniss, National Portrait Gallery. Page 58: Gerard Hoffnung, *HOFFNUNG SYMPHONY ORCHESTRA* (Dobson, 1955), Souvenir Press /Annette Hoffnung. Page 59: *top*, from the *PIPE CLUB OF LONDON JOURNAL*, December 1993; *bottom*, Craven Hill, *PUNCH*. Page 60: Pipe Smokers Council. Page 61: *top*, from *PETIT COURRIER DES DAMES*, 1839; *centre*, Roy Davis; *bottom*, from Bestelmeier's catalogue in *AN ILLUSTRATED HISTORY OF TOYS*. Page 62: from Count Corti, *A HISTORY OF SMOKING* (Harrap, 1931); *bottom*, Briar Pipe Trade Association. Page 64: Pipe Smokers Council. Page 66: Hulton-Deutsch. Page 67: *top left and centre*, Gallaher, *LIVE IN PEACE*; *bottom*, Veldeman Cois, Olen, *KARTOENBOEK*. Page 68: James R Rhodes, *TOM DUNN'S EPHEMERIS*. Page 69: *top*, Weingott; *centre*, Pipe Smokers Council; *bottom*, from A Tindal Hart, *THE CURATE'S LOT*, 1970, in Lambeth Palace Library. Page 70: 'Phiz' in the Household Edition of Charles Dickens, *PICKWICK PAPERS* (Chapman & Hall, 1836). Page 71: *top*, Pipe Smokers Council; *bottom left*, Count Corti, *A HISTORY OF SMOKING* (Harrap, 1931); *bottom right*, Pipe Smokers Council. Page 72: 'Ape', *VANITY FAIR*, 1871, National Portrait Gallery. Page 73: *PUNCH*, 1919. Page 75: *top*, *PUNCH*; bottom, from *NEW FLAME*. Page 76: *bottom*, *PUNCH*, Mary Evans Picture Library. Page 77: from *NEW FLAME*. Page 78: *top*, Bernard Partridge, *PUNCH*, Mary Evans Picture Library; *bottom*, Pipe Smokers Council. Page 79: *B.A.T.*

BULLETIN. Page 80: H M Bateman/ Heather Jeeves. Page 81: *top*, Simpsons; *bottom left*, De Valck Pol (Brasser), Schepdaal, *KARTOENBOEK*; *bottom right*, Wicking. Page 82: *top*, Gallaher, *LIVE IN PEACE*; *bottom*, *THE WALL STREET JOURNAL*, 25 February 1992. Page 83: *top*, *PUNCH*; *bottom*, Count Corti, *A HISTORY OF SMOKING* (Harrap, 1931). Page 84: Stephen Potter, *THE COMPLETE UPMANSHIP* (Rupert Hart-Davis, 1974). Page 85: *top*, Gallaher, *HAMLET MOMENTS*; *bottom*, Frank Holmes (Quanda). Page 86: *top*, Pipe Smokers Council; *bottom*, Charles Sinclair. Page 87: *top*, from Groucho Marx & R J Anobile, *THE MARX BROTHERS SCRAPBOOK* (W H Allen); *bottom*, from The Cinema Bookshop, Great Russell Street. Page 88: from David Robinson, *CHAPLIN HIS LIFE & ART* (Collins, 1985), Roy Export Co Establishment, Lawrence Wright Music Co. Page 89: *bottom*, The Cinema Bookshop. Page 90: Hulton-Deutsch. Page 91: *top*, Bill Caldwell, *DAILY STAR*; *bottom*, Ruskin Spear, 1974, Cavendish Press, National Portrait Gallery. Page 92: *top*, Wally Fawkes ('Trog'), Pipe Smokers Council; *centre*, © Quiller Press 1984; *bottom*, Tony Wysand, 1934, National Portrait Gallery. Page 93: *top*, from *NEW FLAME*; *bottom*, *PUNCH*, 1899. Page 94: *top*, *THE GUARDIAN*; *bottom*, G Steiner/*THE WASHINGTON TIMES*, 14 September 1989. Page 95: Guildhall Library, Corporation of London. Page 96: *top*, Pipe Smokers Council; *centre left*, Brad Anderson/ Knight Features; *centre right*, Heath/*THE SPECTATOR/PRIVATE EYE*; *bottom*, Pipe Smokers Council. Page 97; *top*, E H Shepherd from Rawle Knox, *THE WORK OF E H SHEPHERD* (Methuen, 1979); *bottom*, Don Orehek/*DAILY NEWS MAGAZINE*. Pages 98 and 99: J Wix & Sons/Gallaher. Page 100: *top*, W D & H O Wills/BAT; *bottom*, Kensitas/Gallaher. Page 101: Wills Capstan/BAT. Page 102: Guildhall Library, Corporation of London. Page 103: *top*, Gallaher, *HAMLET MOMENTS*; *bottom*, Kenneth Bird ('Fougasse') from Bevis Hillier (ed), *FOUGASSE* (Hamish Hamilton, 1977). Page 104: from the collection of B C W Heard, one-time editor of *TOBACCO*. Page 105: *top*, Wills/BAT; *bottom*, Guildhall Library, Corporation of London. Pages 106, 107, 108, 109: from the cigarette card collection of Edward Wharton-Tigar. Page 110: Nigel Parry/ Katz Pictures/*TELEGRAPH MAGAZINE*. Pages 111, 112 & 113: Gallaher/Hamlet TV ads. Page 113, *bottom*, from Milbourne Christopher, *THE ILLUSTRATED HISTORY OF MAGIC* (Robert Hale, 1975). Page 114: *top*, Bill Caldwell/Gallaher, *HAMLET MOMENTS*; *bottom*, Jacky Fleming from *NEVER GIVE UP* (Penguin, 1992). Page 115: Nicholas Bentley in J B Morton (Beachcomber), *STUFF & NONSENSE* (Jonathan Cape, 1935). Pages 117 and 118: *PUNCH*. Page 119: *top*, Gerard Hoffnung, *THE HOFFNUNG SYMPHONY ORCHESTRA* (Dobson, 1955), Souvenir Press/Annette Hoffnung; *centre*, *B.A.T. BULLETIN*, 1925; *bottom*, from *RIPPING YARNS* (The Five Mile Press, Balwyn, Victoria, Australia). Page 120 and Page 121, *top and bottom*: W Heath Robinson, The Estate of Mrs J C Robinson. Page 121: *centre*, Pipe Smokers Council. Page 122: *top*, Frank Reynolds, *PUNCH*; bottom, 'Phiz', *PICKWICK PAPERS*. Page 123: *top*, Gallaher, *LIVE IN PEACE*; *centre and bottom*, Hulton-Deutsch. Page 124: *top*, G L Stampa, *PUNCH*, 1919; *bottom*, Fiddy, Gallaher, *HAMLET MOMENTS*. Page 126: *left*, Chris Woodward, London Palladium Theatre Collection; *right*, Milbourne Christopher, *THE ILLUSTRATED HISTORY OF MAGIC* (Robert Hale, 1975). Page 127; *top*,

Chris Woodward; *bottom,* Milbourne Christopher. Pages 129 and 130: Gallaher. Page 131: *New York Observer,* 23 November 1991. Page 132: Gallaher/*Hamlet Moments.* Page 133: Edward Lear. Page 134: Harris, *Lexicon Technicum,* 1704. Page 135: W Heath Robinson, Estate of Mrs J C Robinson. Page 136: *top.* Hulton-Deutsch; *bottom,* Vicky, 1962, from John Geipel, *The Cartoon* (David & Charles, 1972). Page 137: *top,* Haldane/Gallaher, *Hamlet Moments*; *bottom,* Parker, *New York Post,* 7 November 1991. Page 138: *top,* Guildhall Library, Corporation of London; *bottom,* Albert Ellery Berg, *The Drama,* 1884. Page 139: *top,* Nicholas Bentley from Beachcomber, *Stuff & Nonsense*; *bottom,* Barsatti © 1989 *USA Today.* Distributed by L.A. Times Syndicate. Page 140: John Witt. Page 142: Benian (Ian Bennett).

Permission to use stills from Hamlet tv ads from Gallaher's advertising agents Collett, Dickenson, Pearse & Partners (Simon North); and actors Preston Lockwood and Ronnie Corbett.

Every effort has been made to contact the copyright owners of illustrations. The publishers request any owner of the copyright of work reproduced here, whom they have been unable to find, to get in touch without delay.

Index